ESSENTIAL ELEMENTS 2000

FOR STRINGS

A COMPREHENSIVE STRING METHOD

MICHAEL ALLEN • ROBERT GILLESPIE • PAMELA TELLEJOHN HAYES
ARRANGEMENTS BY JOHN HIGGINS

ESSENTIAL ELEMENTS INCLUDES:

Comprehensive Pedagogy
• Address the *process* of teaching and learning.

Melodic Approach
• Early pizzicato tunes develop ear and hand.

Integrated Curriculum
• Theory, history, and multiculturalism in the examples.

Innovative Rhythm System
• Graphics, subdivision, and easy-to-learn sequence.

Easy Note Reading
• Easy notes thoroughly reinforced with note names.

Broad Musical Spectrum
• Classics to contemporary-designed to motivate.

AVAILABLE PUBLICATIONS

Violin
Viola
Cello
Double Bass
Piano Accompaniment
Play-Along CDs
EE String Orchestra Series

ISBN 0-634-03816-8

HAL•LEONARD®
CORPORATION

7777 W. BLUEMOUND RD. P.O. BOX 13819 MILWAUKEE, WI 53213

TABLE OF CONTENTS

The *Essential Elements 2000 for Strings* Teacher's Manual Book 1 is designed to serve as a resource for all your string teaching needs. It contains teaching tips for every page of *Essential Elements 2000 for Strings* Book 1. It also includes sample letters for communicating with parents, sample test forms for evaluating students' playing skills, guidelines for instrument care, sizing students for instruments, a keyboard chart, and words to the some of the familiar melodies throughout the book. National standards for teaching strings as well as a resource list of additional materials to help you in your teaching are provided.

Student Page	Topic/Title	Teacher Page
	Sequence of Essential Elements 2000 Chart	6-9
	Using Essential Elements 2000 for Strings	10-11
	Starting Systems, Rhythm Raps, Play-Along CD Disc 1	10
	Performance Spotlights, EE Skill Builders	10
	Music Theory, History, and Cross-Curricular Activities	10
	Creativity, Assessment, Additional Resources	11
	Essential Elements 2000 for Strings Beginning Skills Teaching Sequence	12
	Parent Communication & Student Evaluation	13-33
1	**History of the Instruments**	34
2	**Parts of the Instrument and Bow**	35-36
3	**Holding Your Instrument**	37-38
4	1. Tuning Track	39
	2. Let's Play "Open D"	40
	3. Let's Play "Open A"	40
	4. Two's A Team	41
	5. At Pierrot's Door	41
5	**Definitions (Clef, Time Signature, Double Bar)**	42
	6. Jumping Jacks	43
	7. Mix 'Em Up	43
	8. Count Carefully	44
	9. Essential Elements Quiz	45
6	**Shaping The Left Hand/D String Notes**	46-47
	Listening Skills	48
	10. Let's Read "G"	49
	11. Let's Read "F♯"	50
	12. Lift Off	51
7	**Shaping The Right Hand**	52-53
	Bow Builder One: Pencil Hold	52-53
	13. On The Trail	54
	14. Let's Read "E"	54
	15. Walking Song	55
	16. Essential Elements Quiz	56
8	**Bow Builder Two: Pencil Hold Exercises**	56-57
	Bow Builder Three: Bowing Motions	56-57
	17. Hop Scotch	57
	18. Morning Dance	58
	19. Rolling Along	59
9	**Work-Outs/Bass: New Note**	60-61
	20. Good King Wenceslas	61
	21. Seminole Chant	62
	22. Essential Elements Quiz – Lightly Row	63
10	**A String Notes (Bass: G String Notes)/Listening Skills**	64-65
	23. Let's Read "D"	66
	24. Let's Read "C♯"	67
	25. Take Off	67
	26. Caribbean Island	68
11	27. Olympic High Jump	69
	28. Let's Read "B"	70
	29. Half Way Down	71
	30. Right Back Up	72
	31. Down The D Scale	73
	32. Essential Elements Quiz – Up The D Scale	74

12   **Bow Builder Four: On The Bow** 75
    33. Song For Christine 76
    34. Natalie's Rose 77
    35. Essential Creativity 78

13   36. Dreidel 79-80
    Bow Builder Five: Shadow Bowing 81
    37. Rosin Rap #1 82
    38. Rosin Rap #2 82
    39. Rosin Rap #3 82

14   40. Carolina Breeze 83
    41. Jingle Bells 84-85
    42. Old MacDonald Had A Farm 86-87

15   43. A Mozart Melody 88-89
    44. Matthew's March 90
    45. Christopher's Tune 91
    46. Essential Creativity 92

16   **Bow Builder Six: Let's Bow!/Listening Skills** 93-95
    47. Bow On The D String 96
    48. Bow On The A String 97

17   **String Levels** 98
    49. Raise And Lower 98-99
    50. Teeter Totter 99
    51. Mirror Image 100
    52. A Strand Of D'N'A 100
    53. Essential Elements Quiz – Olympic Challenge 101
    Bow Builder Seven: Combining Both Hands 102

18   **Putting It All Together** 103
    54. Bowing "G" 103
    55. Back And Forth 104
    56. Down And Up 104
    57. Tribal Lament 105
    58. Bowing "D" 105
    59. Little Steps 106
    60. Elevator Down 106

19   61. Elevator Up 107
    62. Down The D Major Scale 108
    63. Scale Simulator 109
    64. Essential Elements Quiz – The D Major Scale 110-111
    Special Violin, Viola, Cello Exercise 111
    65. Let's Read "C#" – Review 112

20   66. Rhythm Rap 113
    67. Pepperoni Pizza 113
    68. Rhythm Rap 114
    69. D Major Scale Up 114
    70. Hot Cross Buns 115
    71. Au Claire De La Lune 115

21   72. Rhythm Rap 116
    73. Buckeye Salute 116-117
    74. Rhythm Rap 117
    75. Two By Two 118
    76. Essential Elements Quiz – For Pete's Sake 119

22   77. Rhythm Rap 120
    78. At Pierrot's Door 120
    79. The Half Counts 121
    80. Grandparent's Day 122
    81. Michael Row The Boat Ashore 123
    82. Texas Two-String 124

23   **Violin/Viola: 4th Finger/Bass: New Notes** 125
    83. Four By Four 126
    84. 4th Finger Marathon 127
    85. High Flying 127
    86. Essential Elements Quiz – Ode To Joy 128-129

24   **Performance Spotlight**
    87. Scale Warm-Up 130
    88. Frère Jacques – Round 131
    89. Bile 'Em Cabbage Down-Orchestra Arrangement 132-133

25	90. English Round	133
	91. Lightly Row – Orchestra Arrangement	134-135
	92. Can-Can – Orchestra Arrangement	136-137
26	**G String Notes (Bass: E and A String Notes)/Listening Skills**	138-139
	93. Let's Read "G"	140
	94. Let's Read "C"	141
	95. Let's Read "B"	141
	96. Let's Read "A"	142
	97. Walking Around	143
27	98. G Major Scale	144
	99. Fourth Finger D	145
	100. Low Down	146
	101. Baa Baa Black Sheep	147-148
	102. Essential Elements Quiz – This Old Man	149
28	**¾ Time Signature**	150
	103. Rhythm Rap	150
	104. Counting Threes	151
	105. D Major Scale In Threes	151
	106. French Folk Song	152-153
	107. Essential Elements Quiz – Sailor's Song	153-154
29	108. Fit To Be Tied	155
	109. Stop And Go	156
	110. Slurring Along	157
	111. Smooth Sailing	158
	112. D Major Slurs	159
	113. Crossing Strings	160
	114. Gliding Bows	160
	115. Upside Down	161
30	116. Song For Maria	162
	117. Banana Boat Song	163
	118. Firoliralera – Orchestra Arrangement	164-166
31	**EE Skill Builders – G Major**	
	119–124	167-170
	125. Jingli Nona	171-172
32	**New Note: F♮/Listening Skills**	172-173
	126. Let's Read "F"	174
	127. Half-Steppin' And Whole Steppin'	175
	128. Spy Guy	176
	129. Minor Details	177
33	**New Note: C♮/Listening Skills**	178-179
	130. Let's Read "C"	179
	131. Half Step And Whole Step Review	180
	132. Chromatic Moves	180-181
	133. The Stetson Special	181
	134. Bluebird's Song	182
34	135. C Major Scale – Round	183
	136. Split Decision – Duet	184-185
	137. Oak Hollow	186
	138. A-Tisket, A-Tasket	187
	139. Essential Elements Quiz – Russian Folk Tune	188-189
35	140. Bingo	190
	141. Tallis Cannon – Round	191
	142. Variations On A Familiar Song	192-193
	143. Essential Creativity – The Birthday Song	194
36	**Special Violin And Bass Exercise/Listening Skills**	195-196
	144. Let's Read "C"	197
	145. Let's Read "F"	197
	146. Let's Read "E"	198
	147. Let's Read "D"	198
	148. Side By Side	199
	149. C Major Scale	200

37   150. Rhythm Rap 201
       151. Slow Bows 201
       152. Long, Long Ago 202
       153. C Major Scale And Arpeggio 203
       154. Listen To Our Sections 204
       155. Monday's Melody 204-205

38   **Violin/Bass: E String Notes, Viola: E/Listening Skills** 206-207
       156. Let's Read "E" 208
       157. Let's Read "A" 209
       158. Let's Read "G" 209
       159. Let's Read "F♯" 210
       160. Moving Along 211
       161. G Major Scale 212

39   162. Shepherd's Hey 213
       163. Big Rock Candy Mountain 213-214
       164. Let's Read "B" 215
       165. Ice Skating 216
       166. Essential Elements Quiz – Academic Festival Overture Theme 217

40   167. Play Staccato 218
       168. Arkansas Traveler 219
       EE Skill Builders – G Major
       169–173 220-222

41   174. Hooked On D Major 223-224
       175. Waltzing Bows 224-225
       176. Pop Goes The Weasel 225-226
       EE Skill Builders – C Major
       177–180 227-228

42   181. Forte And Piano 229
       182. Surprise Symphony Theme 230-231
       EE Skill Builders – Scales And Arpeggios
       183–187 231-233

43   **Performance Spotlight**
       188. Cripple Creek - Orchestra Arrangement 234-235
       189. Tekele Lomaria – Orchestra Arrangement 236-237

44   **Performance Spotlight**
       190. William Tell Overture – Orchestra Arrangement 238-241
       191. Rockin' Strings – Orchestra Arrangement 242-243

45   **Performance Spotlight**
       192. Simple Gifts – Orchestra Arrangement 244-249

46   193. Solo with Piano Accompaniment
       Violin – Minuet No. 1 250
       Viola – Minuet In C 251
       Cello – Minuet No. 2 252
       Double Bass – March In D 253

47   194. Rhythm Jam 254
       195. Instant Melody 255

       Fingering Chart
       Violin 256
       Viola 256
       Cello 257
       Double Bass 257

48   **EE Reference Index** 258

       Tips for Caring for Your Instrument: What to Do and What Not to Do! 259

       Guidelines for Selecting the Correct Sized String Instrument for Your Students 260

       Keyboard Chart 261

       Words to Familiar Melodies 262

       ASTA with NSOA-Standards for Successful School String/Orchestra Teaching 263-265

       ASTA with the NSOA-Essential Resource List for String Teachers 266

SEQUENCE OF

Teacher Page	34	35–36	37–38	39–41	42–45	46–51	52–56	56–59	60–63	64–68	69–74	75–78
Student Page	1	2	3	4	5	6	7	8	9	10	11	12
Bowings							Bow Builder One: Shaping the Right Hand, Pencil Hold	Bow Builder Two: Pencil Hold Exercises, Bow Builder Three: Bowing Motions				Bow Builder Four: Shaping the Hand on the Bow
Rhythms				♩ 𝄽								
Theory											Scale	
History	Instrument Histories							Folk Songs				
Terms			pizz.	Beat, Music Staff, Bar Line, Measure, Notes, Rest	Clef, Time Signature, Double Bar, Repeat Sign, Counting	Sharp, Keeping Fingers Down Bracket ⎵ (Bass)			Keeping Fingers Down Bracket ⎵ (Violin, Viola, Cello)			
Listening Skills						G, F♯, E				D, C♯, B		
Familiar Melodies				At Pierrot's Door				Morning Dance, Rolling Along	Good King Wenceslas, Lightly Row			
Special Features	Welcome to String Playing	Instrument Care, Instrument Parts, Bow Parts, Accessories	Instrument Position, Pizzicato		Counting Introduced	Shaping Left Hand Introduced			New Bass Note: A on G String, Left Hand Rote Exercises		Pizzicato D Major Scale, Bass Shifting	
Quiz Assessments					pizz. D/A Strings, Counting, ♩ 𝄽 Steady Beat		pizz. D String (G String Bass), Counting, Steady Beat, Square 1st Finger, Time Signature, Clef, Double Bar		pizz. D String (G String Bass), Counting, Steady Beat, Square 1st Finger, Keeping Fingers Down, Violin/Viola Shoulder Position	A String Notes	Left Hand Shape, Bass Shifting, pizz. D Major Scale	Essential Creativity, Drawing Notes on the Staff
Note Sequence												

Correlating St. Orch. Arr. Levels

ESSENTIAL ELEMENTS 2000

Teacher page	79–82	83–87	88–92	93–97	98–102	103–106	107–112	113–115	116–119	120–124	125–129	130–133
Student page	13	14	15	16	17	18	19	20	21	22	23	24
Bowings	Bow Builder Five: Bowing with Rosin Raps			Bow Builder Six: Let's Bow!	String Levels / Bow Builder Seven: Bowing Notes of the D Major Scale	Bowing Fingered Notes						
Rhythms								(rhythm)	(rhythm)	(rhythm)		
Theory		Writing D Major Scale Notes	D Major Key Signature						Time Signature: 2/4, 1st and 2nd Endings	Repeat Signs		Round, Chord, Harmony
History	Israeli Folk Song		Mozart								Beethoven	
Terms	Down Bow, Up Bow			arco	Bow Lift			Tempo Markings: Allegro Moderato Andante				Measure Number
Listening Skills				Bowing Open D, A Strings								
Familiar Melodies	Dreidel	Jingle Bells, Old MacDonald Had A Farm	Twinkle, Twinkle, Little Star					Hot Cross Buns, Au Clair De La Lune		At Pierrot's Door, Grandparent's Day, Michael Row The Boat Ashore	Ode To Joy	Frère Jacques, Bile `Em Cabbage Down
Special Features			Essential Creativity: Composing			Steps For Practicing Music that is Bowed	Special Exercises (Violin, Viola, Cello), Bass C# on A String		Conducting Pattern	4th Finger Pizzicato (Violin, Viola)	Bowing 4th Finger (Violin, Viola)	Performance Spotlight
Quiz Assessments					Parallel Bowing, Smooth and Even Tone, Arm Level Changes at String Crossings		Bowing D/A Notes, Bow Markings, Parallel Bowing, String Levels, Half and Whole Steps		Bow Markings, Parallel Bowing, String Levels, Half and Whole Steps, 1st and 2nd Endings		4th Finger (Violin, Viola)	

Note Sequence — Violin, Viola, Cello, Bass

Correlating Full Orch. Arr. Levels — Explorer Level

SEQUENCE OF

	133–137	138–142	143–149	150–154	155–161	162–166	167–172	173–177	178–182	183–189	190–194	195–200
Teacher Page	133–137	138–142	143–149	150–154	155–161	162–166	167–172	173–177	178–182	183–189	190–194	195–200
Student Page	25	26	27	28	29	30	31	32	33	34	35	36
Bowings		Bowing G String (Violin, Viola, Cello), Bowing E, A Strings (Bass)		Changing Bow Speeds	Slur 2 Notes ♪⌣♪		Slur 3 Notes ♪♪♪					
Rhythms												
Theory		G Major	Common Time $\mathbf{C}$	𝅗𝅥.	Tie, Slur	Upbeat, D.C. al Fine		♮ Half Step, Whole Step	Chromatics	C Major Key Signature	Theme and Variations	
History	Offenbach Operetta					Latin American Music	Far Eastern Music			Nationalistic Music	16th Century, Thomas Tallis	
Terms		Ledger Lines (Violin)								Duet		
Listening Skills			G, A, B, C					F♮	C♮			C String Notes (Viola, Cello)
Familiar Melodies	Lightly Row, Can-Can		Baa Baa Black Sheep, This Old Man	French Folk Song, Sailor's Song		Banana Boat Song, Firoliralera	Jingli Nona		Bluebird's Song	A-Tisket, A-Tasket, Russian Folk Tune	Bingo, Skip To My Lou, Happy Birthday	
Special Features	Performance Spotlight		Writing G Major Notes, 4th Finger D on G String (Violin, Viola), Conducting 4-Beat Pattern	Time Signature: 3/4, Conducting 3-Beat Pattern, New Position II ½ (Bass)		Orchestra Arrangement	EE Skill Builders: G Major	New Finger Pattern: Low 2nd Finger on D String (Violin, Viola)	New Finger Pattern: Low 2nd Finger on A String (Violin, Viola)	Duet, New Position II (Bass)	Low and High Second Finger Patterns (Violin, Viola), Essential Creativity: Creating Rhythms, Round	Special Exercise and Orchestra Team Work, C Major Scale
Quiz Assessments			G String Notes (Violin, Viola, Cello), 4th Finger on G String (Violin, Viola), Counting ♪, 𝅗𝅥 in 4/4 Time	3/4 Time, Counting 𝅗𝅥., Changing Bow Speeds						F-natural C-natural (Violin, Viola), 4th Finger, Tempo Marking: Andante		

Note Sequence

Violin

Viola

Cello

Bass

Correlating St. Orch. Arr. Levels

▲ **Performer Level**

ESSENTIAL ELEMENTS 2000

	201–205	206–212	213–217	218–222	223–228	229–233	234–237	238–243	244–249	250–253	254–257	258
Teacher page	201–205	206–212	213–217	218–222	223–228	229–233	234–237	238–243	244–249	250–253	254–257	258
Student page	37	38	39	40	41	42	43	44	45	46	47	48
Bowings	Changing Bow Speed			♩.	♩♩	Forte Bowing, Piano Bowing						
Rhythms												
Theory	o – Arpeggio										Improvisation	
History							African Music	Gioachino Rossini				
Terms				Staccato	Hooked Bowing	Dynamics			Solo			
Listening Skills		D, E, F♮, F#, G, A	Bowing E String (Violin)									
Familiar Melodies	Long, Long Ago, Monday's Melody		Shepherd's Hey, Big Rock Candy Mountain, Academic Festival Overture Theme	Arkansas Traveler	Pop Goes The Weasel	Surprise Symphony Theme	Cripple Creek	William Tell Overture	Simple Gifts			
Special Features		Upper Octave G Major Scale (Violin)		Staccato, EE Skill Builders: G Major	Hooked Bowing, EE Skill Builders: C Major	Dynamics: *f*, *p*, EE Skill Builders: Scales and Arpeggios	Performance Spotlight, Orchestra Arrangement	Performance Spotlight, Orchestra Arrangement	Performance Spotlight, Orchestra Arrangement	Performance Spotlight, Solo with Piano Accompaniment Violin: Bach Minuet No. 1 Viola: Bach Minuet in C Cello: Bach Minuet No. 2 Bass: Bach March in D	Improvising Rhythms and Melodies, Fingering Chart	EE Reference Index
Quiz/Assessments			E String Notes, Up-Beat									

Note Sequence — Violin, Viola, Cello, Bass (musical notation)

Correlating w/ Orch. Arr. Levels — ▲ Artist Level

USING ESSENTIAL ELEMENTS 2000 FOR STRINGS

Essential Elements 2000 for Strings is a comprehensive method for string musicians, and can be used with hetero-geneous and like-instrument classes or individuals. It is designed with fail-safe options for teachers to customize the learning program to meet their changing needs.

The Teacher's Manual includes all the music and text from the student books, plus time-saving **EE Teaching Tips** throughout the score. As in the student books, the introduction of a new concept is always highlighted by a **color** box.

STARTING SYSTEMS

INSTRUMENT POSITION

- Guitar Position
- Shoulder Position

SHAPING THE LEFT HAND

- Higher numbered fingers first to help shape the hand
- Pizzicato reinforced first so that bowing skills may be developed separately for mastery before combining with left hand skills
- *Work-outs* – rote activities for developing left hand skills

LISTENING SKILLS

- Included for each new pitch to develop intonation skills.

BOW BUILDERS

- Seven carefully sequenced activities for developing string students' beginning bowing skills.

RHYTHM RAPS

After establishing the quarter note pulse, all new rhythms are presented in the innovative **Rhythm Rap** format. Each Rhythm Rap may be clapped, tapped, counted aloud or silently, shadow bowed (bowed in the air), or bowed on an open string. After each Rhythm Rap, the identical rhythms are played on simple pitches in the next exercise.

PLAY-ALONG CD DISC 1

Every student receives a play-along CD in their book tha covers the first 71 exercises. From the very beginning, the can model tone production and technique by listening t a professional orchestra.

For classroom use, the Teacher's Manual includes a play along CD featuring the same exercises, with a small strin ensemble demonstrating the melody part.

Each track is played twice—the second time is the accom paniment only. There is a one measure count-off befor each track, with metronome clicks that are subdivide by soft cymbal notes. These tracks are performed on rea instruments that support phrasing and dynamics, teachin musicality from the start. They explore a rich variety of musica styles and cultures, including classical, rock, jazz, countr and world music.

PERFORMANCE SPOTLIGHTS

Carefully selected music that reviews skills and techniqu and may be used for concert performance.

EE SKILL BUILDERS

Technical exercises to reinforce important playing skills.

MUSIC THEORY, HISTORY, AND CROSS-CURRICULAR ACTIVITIES

All the necessary materials are woven into the learnin program—right in the student books. With teaching tim in short supply, it would normally be impractical to tak class time to relate music to history, world cultures or t other subjects in the curriculum. But *Essential Elements 200 for Strings* correlates these activities with the concepts an music throughout the program. These Theory and Histor features are highlighted by **color** boxes and appea throughout the book.

As a result, teachers can efficiently meet and exceed th **National Standards for Arts Education**, while still havin the time to focus on music performance skills.

CREATIVITY

Essential Creativity exercises appear throughout the book. These are preliminary activities designed to stimulate imaginations, and to foster a creative attitude toward music. Strategies for completing each Essential Creativity exercise are included in the student book. Additional suggestions are included in the Teacher's Manual.

ASSESSMENT

ESSENTIAL ELEMENTS QUIZZES

Playing quizzes appear throughout the student books. Objectives highlight the exact elements being reviewed and tested. Review exercises in the Teacher's Manual suggest specific examples for students requiring additional practice. Be certain students meet your performance expectations on each quiz.

A Star Achiever chart is provided in the Teacher's Manual. It lists all the Essential Elements Quizzes and Essential Creativity exercises. This chart should be reproduced and distributed to each student.

EE CHECKS ✓

EE Checks appear throughout Essential Elements 2000 for Strings. They are special reminders for students to evaluate the playing skills that have just been introduced.

Additional Resources Available...

PLAY-ALONG CD SET DISC 2 & 3

This set of play-along tracks features a variety of accompaniment styles similar to Disc 1, and includes exercise 72 through the end of Book 1. It features the melody demonstrated by a small string ensemble, followed by the accompaniment only for each exercise. For use by all instruments.

PIANO ACCOMPANIMENT BOOK

Piano accompaniments for each exercise are provided in a separate book, but are also printed in the Teacher's Manual. These easy accompaniments have been arranged to match the style and harmony of the accompaniments heard on the play-along CDs. They may be used for teaching or performance and offer a variety of styles, from classical to contemporary popular music. You may want to alter these piano accompaniments to meet your specific needs.

CORRELATED MATERIALS

The Essential Elements 2000 for String Series includes original and popular music, arranged for beginning strings. Each publication is correlated to one of five specific "levels" within Books 1 and 2 (see the Sequence Of Essential Elements 2000 chart in the Teacher's Manual for details). Contact your music dealer or the publisher for information on the latest releases in this series.

ESSENTIAL ELEMENTS 2000 FOR STRINGS BEGINNING SKILLS TEACHING SEQUENCE

Beginning string students need to learn many different skills when first learning to play their string instruments: Left Hand (posture, instrument position, left hand shape, and finger dexterity), and Right Hand (bow hand shape and detache bowing). Each of these skills needs to be introduced separately, and then developed simultaneously. *Essential Elements 2000 for Strings* is designed so that students can learn each of these skills sequentially and independently, leading to mastery. For ease of reference, the following diagram outlines the introduction and integration of each of these skills.

Left Hand Skills

Instrument Position, pg. 3

Left Hand Shape D string
pizz. G, F♯ pg. 6

pizz. G, F♯, E, D pg. 7

pizz. A string notes
pizz. D,C♯, pg. 10

pizz. D Major Scale pitches, pg. 11

Right Hand Skills

Bow Builder One:
Shaping the Right Hand, pg. 7

Bow Builder Two:
Pencil Hold Exercises, pg. 9
Shaping the bow hand on a pencil

Bow Builder Three:
Bowing Motions, pg. 9
Learning bowing motions in the air

practicing Bow Builders
One, Two, and Three, pg. 10

Bow Builder Four:
On the Bow, pg. 12
Holding the Bow

Bow Builder Five:
Shadow Bowing, pg. 13
Bowing on rosin

Practicing Bow Builder Five, pg. 14

Bow Builder Six:
Let's Bow!, pg. 16
Bowing open strings

String Crossings, pg. 17
Changing string levels
On the A and D strings

Bow Builder Seven:
Combining Both Hands, pg. 17
Bowing D Major Scale pitches

PARENT COMMUNICATION & STUDENT EVALUATION

Teacher

Communication with parents is an essential element for a successful orchestra program. The following letters and "Message For Parents" provide valuable information for orchestra parents. Feel free to adapt or make photocopies of these materials for your use. The letters include the following topics:

• Recruiting students

• "Message To Parents" explaining benefits of string study

• Guidelines for obtaining an instrument

• After the first week of study

• After 3–4 weeks of study

• Midyear practice encouragement

• When a student is discouraged or considering dropping out

• Instrument maintenance needed

• When student forgets instrument for class

• Concert Etiquette

• When students are signing up for next year's classes

The evaluation forms and reports include the following:

• Progress Report

• Position Evaluation

• Orchestra Progress Report

• Orchestra Class Interim Report

• Performance Evaluation (2)

• Practice Record

DATELINE: Distribute to all students when recruiting

Dear Parents:

(Name of school or school district) is pleased to be able to offer beginning strings instruction to students in the (grade level) grade this year. Orchestra classes will meet during the school day and will be free of charge. Instruction will be offered on violin, viola, cello, and bass. In order for your child to participate in these classes, it will be necessary for you to furnish an instrument. Local music stores offer very reasonable rental or lease plans for these instruments. Please do not obtain an instrument until your child has received a written notice of the exact instrument needed.

String instrument instruction will continue to be available to your child through the 12th grade. Learning to play an instrument and belonging to the school orchestra opens up a whole new world of friendship and fun. Your child will be able to take advantage of music performances with orchestras at the (middle school or junior high) and high school levels. The opportunities for playing a string instrument after high school are abundant, with many universities offering scholarships for orchestra participation. Orchestra provides a great foundation for your child in all aspects of life. In addition to music, students learn self-discipline, group cooperation, problem-solving, goal-setting, self-expression, memory skills, concentration, poise, enhanced physical coordination, high self-esteem, and the importance of teamwork—skills in great demand in almost every aspect of life. Like all the arts, music has a profound effect on the academic success of students as well.

If you wish to enroll your child, please complete and return the application form to the orchestra teacher at the school. If additional information is desired, please feel free to contact me at (phone number).

Cordially,

Orchestra Teacher

- -

(Please detach and return)

ORCHESTRA APPLICATION FORM

Name_____

Address _____

Phone (Home)_____(Work) _____

Homeroom _____Teacher _____

Parent's Signature_____

DATELINE: Distribute your version of this "Message To Parents" at your first orchestra parents meeting

MESSAGE TO PARENTS
A Parent's Guide To Enhancing Your Child's Musical Experiences

CONGRATULATIONS

Your decision to provide your child with a quality musical instrument is an investment in your child's future. In making it possible for your child to play a musical instrument, you are providing the opportunity for self-expression, creativity, and achievement.

Numerous studies indicate that parental attitude, support and involvement are important factors in a child's ability to successfully learn to play and enjoy music.

These guidelines are designed to assist you in giving your child the best support possible for his or her musical endeavors. Like any skill, interest counts far more than talent. With strong support from you, playing music will become a natural part of your child's life.

BENEFITS

For Your Child
Music participation enhances:
- Problem-solving
- Teamwork
- Goal-setting
- Self-expression
- Physical coordination
- Memory skills
- Self-confidence and esteem
- Concentration
- Poise
- and much, much more!

For Your Family
- A child's music study also offers opportunities for shared family experiences, including:
- Musical event attendance
- Family music-making
- Performing for, and with, family and friends
- Learning about the lives of composers and the cultural heritage of many civilizations
- A sense of accomplishment and pride for the entire family

HOW YOU FIT IN

Always keep in mind that your support is an essential element in your child's success with music study.

Schedule Practice Times
Music achievement requires effort over a period of time. The time in orchestra rehearsal is limited. New concepts learned at school need daily personal practice time by your child at home in order for these new skills to be developed. You can help your child by:
- Providing a quiet place in which to practice
- Remaining nearby during practice times as often as possible
- Scheduling a consistent daily time for practice
- Praising your child's efforts and achievements

WHAT TO DO

To give your child the best possible support, you should:
- Remind your child to bring instrument and music to orchestra class
- Encourage your child to play for family and friends
- Offer compliments and encouragement regularly
- Expose your child to a wide variety of music, including concerts and recitals
- Encourage your child to talk with you about classes
- Make sure your child's instrument is always maintained well
- Listen to your child practice, and acknowledge improvement
- Help your child build a personal music library
- Encourage your child to make a commitment to his or her music studies
- Get to know your child's teacher

WHAT TO AVOID

- Using practice as a punishment
- Insisting your child play for others when he/she doesn't want to
- Ridiculing or making fun of mistakes of less-than-perfect playing
- Apologizing to others for your child's weak performance

TO MAINTAIN YOUR CHILD'S INTEREST

- Talk with your child if his or her interest begins to decline
- Discuss with the orchestra teacher ways to maintain your child's enthusiasm for playing
- Increase your enthusiasm and involvement in your child's playing

CREDITS

This message has been adapted from publications by the following organizations in the interest of making music study and participation an enjoyable and richly rewarding experience for children and their families. Hal Leonard Corporation appreciates the cooperation of these organizations for graciously allowing us to reprint this important message.

AMERICAN MUSIC CONFERENCE
303 East Wacker Drive, Suite 1214
Chicago, IL   60601
(312) 856-8820

MUSIC EDUCATORS NATIONAL CONFERENCE
1806 Robert Fulton Drive
Reston, VA   22091-4348
(703) 860-4000

MUSIC TEACHERS NATIONAL ASSOCIATION
617 Vine St., Suite 1432
Cincinnati, OH 45202-2434
(513) 421-1420

NATIONAL ASSOCIATION OF MUSIC MERCHANTS
5140 Avenida Encinas
Carlsbad, CA 92008-4391
(619) 438-8001

DATELINE: Distribute to students once they have been measured for an instrument

PLEASE TAKE THIS FORM WITH YOU TO THE MUSIC STORE

_____ is officially enrolled in the (name of school) Orchestra Program. An instrument may be obtained from any of our local music stores who have agreed to stock the proper sizes and specifications for our school. These stores have reasonable lease, rental, and/or trial-purchase plans available. You may do business with any store you prefer. They are listed in alphabetical order.

(List names of music stores with addresses, phone numbers, and contact persons)

If you are considering purchasing an instrument from another source, we suggest you call on us to assist you in evaluating it, as one of the principle causes of pupil failure is an inferior instrument. You should obtain the following for your child:

1. Instrument _____ Size _____

2. *Essential Elements 2000 for Strings,* Book I (be sure the book has the same name as the instrument)

3. A folding metal music stand

4. A shoulder pad for violins and viola

5. A rock stop for cellos and basses (sometimes this is included with the instrument)

6. Stool for basses; if needed

7. A pencil - BRING TO EVERY CLASS!

8. A soft cloth to keep the instrument clean

9. Rosin

Students enrolling in orchestra must understand that they are making a commitment to daily practice at home. Good practice habits and a positive attitude have a great effect on the success your child will achieve through this class.

Parents are urged to consult the teacher any time a question or problem arises. The earlier a positive working relationship is reached between child, parent and teacher, the greater your child's success will be.

Sincerely,

Orchestra Teacher

DATELINE: Send first week of the program

Dear Parents:

Congratulations on enrolling your child in the orchestra!   Orchestra is one of the most rewarding and exciting educational opportunities offered by our schools. Your investment will pay tremendous dividends in your child's life for many years to come.

Music provides students with a wealth of benefits. In addition to obtaining the musical skills needed to become a performer, a child learns skills that can be used in every facet of life. Team work, dedication, self-discipline and responsibility prepare a child for a successful future in any profession he/she may choose. A variety of research shows that music students are among the academically strongest in their schools and score higher on the SAT than other students. Most colleges and universities now look for more than good grades on a child's transcript. They want well-rounded students that have been able to accomplish more than textbook knowledge.

You do not have to know anything about music to assist your child in this new endeavor. Arrange a time and place where practice can be done without interruptions. This practice should become a part of each child's daily routine. He/she should never merely put in the required time, but should practice with the goal of always improving. Music should be placed at eye level. Please do not allow your child to put the music on a table, bed, etc. This encourages poor playing posture. Remember, practice doesn't necessarily make perfect, but PERFECT practice does!

Again, I congratulate you on enrolling your child in the orchestra. As the year progresses, I hope you will feel free to contact me whenever necessary.

Sincerely,

Orchestra Teacher

DATELINE: Send 3-4 weeks into the program

Dear Parents:

It is a pleasure to have your child in the (name of school or school district) Orchestra Program. This school district offers string instruction from the (grade level of beginners) through the 12th grade. The program is a continuous one, and I hope to see every student performing in the high school orchestra some day. Your interest and support is a lifetime investment for your child.

All beginning classes are now underway, and I'm sure your child has already performed for you. Proper care of the instrument is encouraged. Students have been shown how to handle the instrument so as not to harm it. I suggest that no one else handle the instrument unless they have your permission and your child's instructions.

During the first several weeks of class the primary emphasis has been on developing good playing position as well as correct posture. Failure to master these concepts can hamper a student's ability and progress for years to come. Thus, these first few weeks are the most critical. This cannot be overemphasized! Practice is needed to develop the coordination and strength necessary to play a stringed instrument. A practice "marathon" cannot accomplish the same results as consistent daily practice. Your encouragement is a very important ingredient for your child's success right now.

Report cards will be sent home every (number) weeks so that you may follow your child's progress. Please encourage (student's name) to demonstrate for you and other supportive family members what he/she has learned and be generous in your praise and encouragement. Help (student's name) to remember his/her instrument and materials for class. A child takes pride not only in learning to play, but in learning to play well.

As questions or problems arise, please feel free to contact me. I hope that your child's experience with the orchestra is a successful one.

Sincerely,

Orchestra Teacher

DATELINE: Send as needed

Dear Parents:

Now that our school year is (nearly halfway completed), I would like to touch base with you regarding your child's participation in the orchestra. We've had a very good year so far, and the orchestra shows a lot of promise. I am very proud of all of the students and the progress they have made.

Keep in mind that the beginning of the year had the excitement of a new instrument and a new activity. Then came the excitement of being able to perform that first tune, followed by the thrill of a public performance complete with lots of applause and proud parents. Now that all of that is gone, we have settled back into the routine of learning to develop new technical skills. Don't be surprised if your child experiences some decrease in interest during this time. It is completely normal. However, with your continued support and encouragement, we can overcome any decline in enthusiasm and reach for the next performance level.

Your child may need EXTRA encouragement during the next few weeks to continue good practice habits and performance in class. These are the formative years and how (he/she) handles situations now can determine the way (he/she) approaches every aspect of life. Though the requirements for learning an instrument often demand a high level of personal discipline, it is this same discipline which will be applied as a habit to all tasks in life, especially (his/her) academic success right now. A child must learn that long range benefits of a task only come from long range commitment and dedication.

Please contact me at your earliest convenience if you would like to discuss any aspect of your child's performance in orchestra class. I am anxious to do all I can to assist you in the successful development of your child's abilities.

Sincerely,

Orchestra Teacher

DATELINE: When a student is discouraged or considering dropping out

Dear (Name of Parent):

I want to express my concern that (name of child) seems to be experiencing some decline in interest in orchestra class. I want you to know that while this is a very normal occurrence, it is important to address immediately. A child experiences a variety of levels of interest during the first year of study. However, it is not common for (him/her) to consider dropping out of the program completely.

As a parent, I ask you for your extra support and encouragement during this time. Do not make a hasty decision, something which you and your child could regret for years to come. Everyone experiences periods of discouragement during (his/her) music study. We all know that it is easy to start a task, but making it to the finish line takes persistence, especially when the going gets rough. I have met countless adults who say, "I wish I hadn't quit" or "I wish I would have had the opportunity to play when I was in school." Of course, there are times when pushing a child too far can have the opposite effect and make the child resentful of music in the future. Neither one of us wants this to happen. There is a fine line between the two, and it is sometimes difficult to distinguish what is best for each child.

Thus, the purpose of this letter is simply to ask that we work together to make the best possible decision for your child's future. Please contact me at your earliest convenience to discuss the matter. I will support whatever decision you feel is best for your child.

Sincerely,

Orchestra Teacher

DATELINE: Send as needed

To the parents of:

_____

      Proper instrument maintenance and equipment is essential for each student. An instrument must be in excellent condition or it will hamper a student's progress. The checklist below is for your assistance. When the necessary items have been corrected, please return this sheet to the instructor.

_____ Clean body of fingerprints, rosin dust, etc. USE ONLY POLISH MADE ESPECIALLY FOR STRINGED INSTRUMENTS WHICH IS AVAILABLE AT A MUSIC STORE.

_____ String(s) need to be replaced.

_____ Bridge needs to be replaced. Please be sure the bridge is properly fitted by a repairman. You must take the instrument with you to the music store. Simply buying a bridge will not solve the problem.

_____ Soundpost must be set-up and adjusted inside the instrument.

_____ A shoulder pad is needed to support the instrument properly. It is suggested that the student take the instrument with him and try out several to find the one that is the most effective.

_____ A rock stop is needed.

_____ The bow needs to be rehaired.

_____ Rosin is needed.

_____ The fine tuner needs to be repaired or replaced.

_____ Repair bass stool as needed.

_____ A cloth is needed to keep in the case. (Any soft cloth will work.)

_____ Other:

      Remember to have your child return this letter to me when the above item(s) have been corrected. If you need further information, please feel free to contact me.

                                    Sincerely,

                                    Orchestra Teacher

Date notified: _____

Date corrected: _____

Parent's Signature _____

DATELINE: Send when student forgets instrument for class

Dear parents:

Your child was without an instrument in orchestra class today. In an effort to assure that he/she does not fall behind in class, I asked your child to make detailed notes of the material covered during class. It is important for your child to practice this material at home today so that his/her grade will not be affected. Please have your child return this paper with your signature tomorrow.

Sincerely,

Orchestra Teacher

Parent's Signature _____

CLASS NOTES (use back if needed):

DATELINE: Send before concerts-Concert Etiquette

Dear Parents:

   The students have made great progress in learning the fundamentals of playing their string instrument. They are so excited to perform for you and friends! As this may be the first time they have ever performed in a formal concert setting, please help them prepare by reviewing these guidelines together for proper concert etiquette. These also include suggestions for audience behavior expectations to help you.

   Date of the concert: (day) _____ , date _____ .

• Students should arrive early enough before the concert begins for tuning and warm-up. Students should arrive at (concert site) _____ by (time) _____ .

• Students should arrive at the concert site in proper concert attire. Clothes should be neat and clean . Boys should wear: _____ ; girls should wear: _____ .

• Be sure your child brings his/her music, instrument, and bow to the concert. The students will be excited, so it will be easy for them to forget.

• Students should sit quietly on stage during the concert and acknowledge applause of the audience as directed by the teacher. During the concert the students should focus their attention on their director. They should avoid looking at the audience. Students should especially watch the director closely for all starting and stopping cues.

• Remind students that it is inappropriate for them to eat, drink, or chew gum during a concert.

• During the concert students should maintain good posture and a positive stage presence at all times when on stage. They are not only representing themselves, but also the entire orchestra.

• Encourage your child to play with his/her best effort. One purpose of a concert is to show the audience the great progress made. Of course, students should must enjoy making beautiful music!

   Thanks so much for letting me teach your child. The children have worked very hard and are eager to perform for you and your family and friends. Maybe your child has already played for you some of the music that will be performed. I look forward to seeing you at the concert!

                                        Sincerely,

                                        Orchestra Teacher

DATELINE: Send when students are signing up for next year's classes

Dear Parents:

I know you share my pride in your child's progress in orchestra this year. The personal discipline and commitment have paid off many times over. We've had a GREAT year!

It is now the time of year when students must schedule classes for the coming year. Make certain that orchestra is part of that schedule. If there is ANY indecision or scheduling problems concerning your child's future participation in the orchestra program, please make an appointment with me so we can discuss this matter. Sometimes it may seem that required courses allow no room for electives, but there are many ways to include orchestra in your child's schedule.

I want your child to enjoy continued positive growth during his/her educational career. Group participation enhances self esteem, and there is nothing that brings out a sense of personal contribution quite like being in the orchestra. You have made a great investment in your child's future, and there are many benefits still ahead.

Again, I encourage your communication in this important step. If you have any questions, please feel free to call me at school (#) or home (#). I am your partner in seeing that your child has the opportunity to continue his/her important musical development.

Sincerely,

Orchestra Teacher

Dear Parents:

After (number of weeks) in orchestra, we have completed (number) pages in *Essential Elements 2000 for Strings* Book 1. We are continuing to have a good year, and I am very proud of our progress. Thank you for all of the support you have offered to this success. What follows is a progress report for your child.

PROGRESS REPORT

Student's Name _____

Letter Grade: _____

	1 = outstanding	2 = above average	3 = average	4 = below average
INSTRUMENT POSITION ———————	1	2	3	4
LEFT HAND POSITION ———————	1	2	3	4
RIGHT HAND POSITION ———————	1	2	3	4
RHYTHM —————————————	1	2	3	4
BOWING SKILLS ————————	1	2	3	4
REMEMBERING EQUIPMENT ————	1	2	3	4

Please check the following:
_____ My child always practices without being reminded.
_____ My child usually practices without being reminded.
_____ My child seldom practices without being reminded.
_____ My child practices only when reminded.
_____ My child seldom practices at all.

Parent's Signature _____

Please have your child return this letter to me when the above report has been completed and signed by you. I would like to remind you about our upcoming concert on (date/time/location). You and your entire family are invited to hear our performance. Thank you again for your support!

Sincerely,

Orchestra Teacher

POSITION EVALUATION

Name _____

SKILL ♪	CHECK LIST ♪
+ Indicates skill is demonstrated	– Indicates skill needs to be improved

Instrument Hold/Posture

_____ Sitting/standing properly

_____ Instrument at correct angle

_____ Instrument properly supported

Bow Hand

_____ Thumb placement

_____ Thumb bent

_____ All fingers placed correctly

_____ Fingers over frog

_____ Pinky curved

Left Hand Position

_____ Fingers properly curved

_____ Thumb placement

_____ No squeezing the neck

_____ Arm/elbow at correct angle

_____ Wrist properly aligned

Comments:

Parent's Signature _____

Orchestra Progress Report
First Grading Period

Student's Name_____

Letter Grade _____

	1 = outstanding	2 = above average	3 = average	4 = below average
INSTRUMENT POSITION ——————	1	2	3	4
LEFT HAND POSITION —————	1	2	3	4
RIGHT HAND POSITION —————	1	2	3	4
BOWING SKILLS ———————	1	2	3	4
REMEMBERING EQUIPMENT ————	1	2	3	4

COMMENTS:

Parent's Signature_____

Orchestra Class Interim Report

Name _____

1 = outstanding   2 = above average   3 = average   4 = below average   5 = failing

CLASS PERFORMANCE   **COMMENTS**

1. Proper care of instrument/music   1   2   3   4   5

2. Remembering equipment   1   2   3   4   5

3. Correct posture   1   2   3   4   5

4. Mastery of daily assignments   1   2   3   4   5

5. Attitude and effort in class   1   2   3   4   5

LEFT HAND-FINGER DEVELOPMENT

1. Position   1   2   3   4   5

2. Intonation   1   2   3   4   5

BOWING DEVELOPMENT

1. Right hand position   1   2   3   4   5

2. Flexibility   1   2   3   4   5

RHYTHM

1. Counts or taps toe during class   1   2   3   4   5

2. Correct rhythms   1   2   3   4   5

3. Steady beat   1   2   3   4   5

GRADE __   **PARENT'S SIGNATURE** _____

Performance Evaluation

Name _____

SKILL	POINTS POSSIBLE	SCORE
Instrument Position	20	_____
Bow Hand Position	20	_____
Left Hand Position	20	_____
Bowing Skills	20	_____
Intonation	20	_____

TOTAL: _____

GRADE: _____

COMMENTS:

Performance Evaluation

Name _____

SKILL	POINTS POSSIBLE	SCORE
Instrument Position	30	_____
Bow Hand Position	15	_____
Bowing Skills	15	_____
Left Hand Position	30	_____
Correct Notes	5	_____
Rhythm	5	_____

TOTAL: _____

GRADE: _____

COMMENTS:

PRACTICE RECORD

Name _____

Week: _____   **DUE:** _____

Assignment: _____

_____

_____

_____

Friday	Saturday	Sunday	Monday	Tuesday	Wednesday	Thursday
☐	☐	☐	☐	☐	☐	☐

(number of minutes each day)

TOTAL for the week: _____   GRADE EARNED _____

Parent's Signature: _____

You can mark your progress through the book on this page. Fill in the stars as instructed by your orchestra teacher.

ESSENTIAL
ELEMENTS
2000
FOR STRINGS
STAR ACHIEVER

NAME _____

1. Page 3, Holding Your Instrument
2. Page 5, EE Quiz, No. 9
3. Page 7, EE Quiz, No. 16
4. Page 9, EE Quiz, No. 22
5. Page 11, EE Quiz, No. 32
6. Page 12, Essential Creativity, No. 35
7. Page 13, Shadow Bowing
8. Page 15, Essential Creativity, No. 46
9. Page 17, EE Quiz, No. 53
10. Page 19, EE Quiz, No. 64
11. Page 21, EE Quiz, No. 76
12. Page 23, EE Quiz, No. 86
13. Pages 24–25, Performance Spotlight
14. Page 27, EE Quiz, No. 102
15. Page 28, EE Quiz, No. 107
16. Page 31, No. 125
17. Page 33, No. 134
18. Page 34, EE Quiz, No. 139
19. Page 35, Essential Creativity, No. 143
20. Page 39, EE Quiz, No. 166
21. Pages 43–46, Performance Spotlight

MUSIC — AN ESSENTIAL ELEMENT OF LIFE

Teacher Discuss with students the key elements in the first paragraph on student book page one. Congratulate students on their decision to play a string instrument. Stress that much of their success as a new musician will depend on the degree and quality of their practice. Point out the life-long learning and playing experiences possible with string instruments. Briefly discuss your musical experiences with string instruments, both as an avocation and career.

A brief instrument history also appears on student book page one. Consider showing students photos of early string instruments. Students like to hear stories about some of the most famous instrument makers such as Guaneri, Amati, and Stradivarius. Also showing photos and playing recordings of famous string instrument performers helps develop students' interests in playing string instruments. Talk about the history of your string instrument and bow.

HISTORY OF THE INSTRUMENTS

Violin

The string family includes the violin, viola, violoncello, and the double bass. The violin dates back to the 16th century. The early ancestors of the violin were the Arabian rebab and rebec, popular during the 14th–16th centuries. During the 1500s, there were two types of viols: the viola da gamba, played on the knee, and the viola da braccia, played on the shoulder.

Gasparo da Salo, an Italian instrument maker, developed the present day violin during the 16th century. Da Salo and Nicolo Amati are credited with establishing the design of today's violin, which has survived with only a few minor changes. Antonio Stradivari, and the Guarneri and Guadagnini families were famous instrument makers from the 17th and 18th centuries, and their violins are still in use today.

Nearly every composer has written music for the violin, including Johann Sebastian Bach, Ludwig van Beethoven, and Peter Illyich Tchaikovsky. Famous violin performers include Midori, Isaac Stern, Stéphane Grapelli, Itzhak Perlman, Jascha Heifetz, Joshua Bell, and Mark O'Connor.

Viola

The string family includes the violin, viola, violoncello, and the double bass. The early ancestors of the string family were the Arabian rebab and rebec, popular during the 14th–16th centuries. The viola is the oldest of the modern string instruments, and the word "viola" was used to describe many different string instruments until the 18th century. Today's violas look like violins, though they are larger and longer.

The sound of the viola includes notes lower than the violin and has a particular mellow quality that is darker and richer. The viola is often referred to as the alto voice of the orchestra. Antonio Stradivari, and the Guarneri and Guadagnini families were famous instrument makers from the 17th and 18th centuries, and their violas are still in use today.

Many important composers have been violists, including Wolfgang Amadeus Mozart and Paul Hindemith. Other composers known for their viola compositions include Hector Berlioz, Ernest Bloch, and Bela Bartok. Famous viola performers include Walter Trampler, Lionel Tertis, Donald McGinnis, and William Primrose.

Cello

The string family includes the violin, viola, violoncello, and the double bass. The early ancestors of the string family were the Arabian rebab and rebec, popular during the 14th–16th centuries. During the 1500s, there were two types of viols: the viola da gamba, played on the knee, and the viola da braccia, played on the shoulder.

The sound of the violoncello, called 'cello' for short, is pitched an octave below the viola. The cello has a warm tone and is capable of playing a wide range of dynamics. It is often referred to as the tenor of the orchestra. Antonio Stradivari, and the Guarneri and Guadagnini families were famous instrument makers from the 17th and 18th centuries, and their cellos are still in use today.

Nearly every composer has written music for the cello, including Johann Sebastian Bach, Ludwig van Beethoven, and Peter Illyich Tchaikovsky. Famous cello performers include Janos Starker, Leonard Rose, Pablo Casals, and Yo Yo Ma.

Bass

The string family includes the violin, viola, violoncello, and the double bass. The double bass (also called the 'string bass', or the 'bass' for short) is the most versatile of all the string instruments. At home in the symphony orchestra, jazz combo, concert band, and the dance band, the double bass provides the harmonic foundation in many styles of music.

The double bass sounds much lower than the cello and is tuned differently than the other instruments of the string family. Gasparo da Salo is credited with being the first to make a double bass in its present form. Other famous double bass makers include Carlo Guiseppe Testore, Carlo Bergonzi, and John Frederich Lott.

Nearly every composer has written music for the double bass, including Johann Sebastian Bach, Ludwig van Beethoven, and Peter Illyich Tchaikovsky. Famous double bass performers include Gary Karr, Francois Rabbath, Ron Carter, Milt Hinton, and Ray Brown.

Teacher **Essential Elements Instructional Design**

Students need to develop mastery of their instrument position, left hand shape, and fingering skills before combining with bowing skills. This method has been designed to develop students' right and left-hand skills simultaneously, but independently. This sequence of learning promotes mastery, and greatly helps your students learn to properly play their string instrument.

The following instructions appear on page 2 of each student book. Review the principal parts of the instruments, and point out the need to handle string instruments carefully. They are fragile and easily damaged. Have students state the name of each instrument part as they are touching it.

Violin

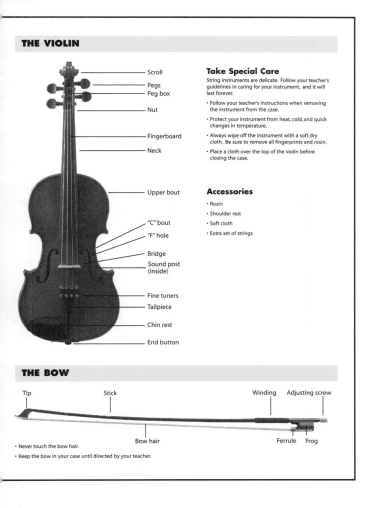

Viola

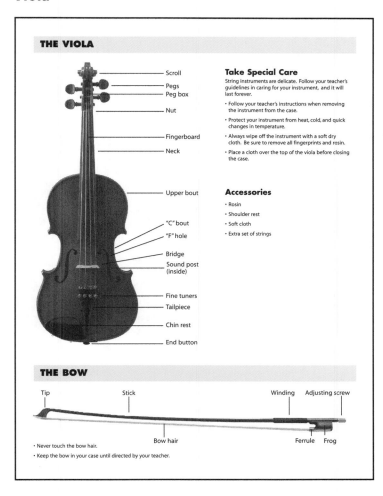

Violin/ Viola Instruct students to leave the bow in their case until they have developed their bow hand shape on a pencil, pen, or straw. Students need to develop mastery of their instrument position, left hand shape, and finger dexterity before combining with bowing skills.

Cello

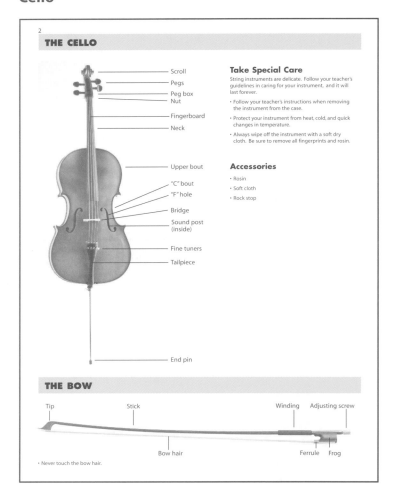

Bass

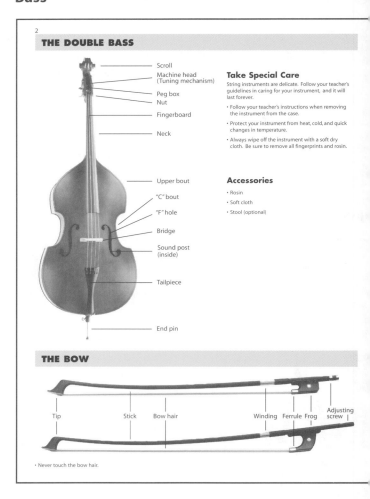

Cello/Bass Instruct students to take the bow out of the case before removing the instrument. This will help protect the bow from being damaged. At the end of class, students should loosen the end pin screw, carefully push the end pin in the instrument, put the instrument in the case, and then return the bow to the case.

Teacher Demonstrate and lead each instrument through the four instrument-position steps on student book page 3. Then lead the students as a class through the four steps. Be sure to carefully check each student's instrument position so that an acceptable instrument position may be established right from the start. Practice leading the students through the four steps many times so that correct instrument position habits may be secured.

Have students compare their posture and instrument position to the drawings on student book page 3. Students may also assist the teacher by comparing their classmates' posture and instrument to the drawings. Actively employing students in the teaching process helps them be aware of their own playing skills.

Violin

Guitar Position   *Shoulder Position*

Viola

Guitar Position   *Shoulder Position*

Violin/ Viola Demonstrate your preferred method of holding the instrument. Many teachers instruct their beginning violin and viola students first to play in guitar position. Playing in guitar position requires fewer specific teacher instructions. This helps students easily pizzicato open strings on the first day of class. Guitar position also enables students to more easily develop their left-hand position separately while they are gradually developing shoulder position playing skills.

Playing in shoulder position is a skill that students develop over a period of time. As students' left-hand shapes are developing in guitar position, begin to gradually introduce shoulder position. When ready, have students first learn how to hold the instrument on their shoulder, and then begin to pizzicato. Be sure students have some type of commercial shoulder pad, or material such as foam rubber, to provide adequate instrument support in shoulder position. There should be friction between the material and the student's clothing to help prevent the instrument from slipping. To determine the proper height of the shoulder pad, a student's jawbone should generally be parallel to the floor when the instrument is in shoulder position. Note that the button of the instrument is positioned at or near the center of the player's neck.

Cello

HOLDING YOUR INSTRUMENT

The best way to learn to play your instrument is to practice one skill at a time. Repeat each step until you are comfortable demonstrating it for your teacher and classmates.

Step 1   Remove the bow from the case and put it in a safe place. Open the case and remove the cello. Identify all parts of the cello.

Step 2   Adjust the length of the end pin so that the scroll of the cello is near your nose when standing.

Step 3   Sit on the front half of your chair with your feet positioned underneath your knees. Place the end pin directly in front of you one arm's length away.

Step 4   Lean the cello slightly to the left and allow the instrument to rest against your chest. The 'C' peg should be near your head behind your left ear, and both knees should touch the cello just below the 'C' bout. It may be necessary to readjust the length or position of the end pin. Identify the letter names of each string: C (lowest pitch), G, D, A. Raise your right index finger over the strings and pluck them as directed by your teacher. Plucking the strings is called *pizzicato*, and is abbreviated *pizz.*

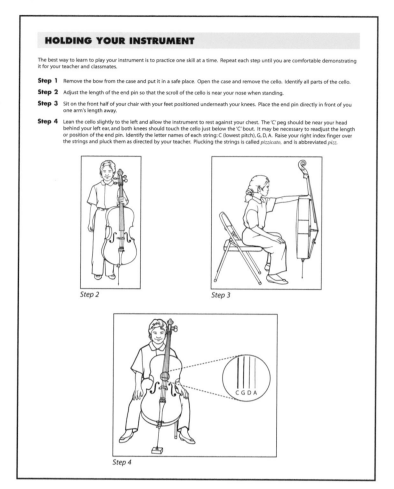

Step 2   Step 3

Step 4

Bass

HOLDING YOUR INSTRUMENT

The best way to learn to play your instrument is to practice one skill at a time. Repeat each step until you are comfortable demonstrating it for your teacher and classmates.

Holding The Double Bass (sitting)

Step 1   Remove the bow from the case and put it in a safe place. Open the case and remove the bass. Identify all parts of the bass.

Step 2   Adjust the length of the end pin so that the nut of the bass is near the top of your forehead when standing.

Step 3   Sit squarely on the front half of the stool with your right foot on the floor and your left foot on a rung of the stool. Place the end pin in front of your left foot about one arm's length away.

Step 4   Rotate the bass slightly to the right and lean the bass toward your body so that the upper bout rests against the left side of your stomach. Identify the letter names of each string: E (lowest pitch), A, D, G. Raise your right index finger over the strings and pluck them as directed by your teacher. Plucking the strings is called *pizzicato*, and is abbreviated *pizz.*

Holding The Double Bass (standing)

Step 1   Remove the bow from the case and put it in a safe place. Open the case and remove the bass. Identify all parts of the bass.

Step 2   Adjust the length of the end pin so that the nut of the bass is near the top of your forehead when standing.

Step 3   Place the end pin in front of your left foot about one arm's length away. Place your left foot slightly forward.

Step 4   Rotate the bass slightly to the right and lean the bass toward your body so that the upper bout rests against the left side of your stomach. Identify the letter names of each string: E (lowest pitch), A, D, G. Raise your right index finger over the strings and pluck them as directed by your teacher. Plucking the strings is called *pizzicato*, and is abbreviated *pizz.*

Bass   Students may play the bass standing or sitting. The authors suggest that beginning students play the bass while sitting on a stool. This helps balance the bass, freeing the player's left hand from holding the bass in the beginning stages of playing. Inexpensive thirty-inch stools may be purchased from local hardware stores for students to use. However, be sure that the length of the legs of the stool allows the player's right foot to rest flat on the floor comfortably. This may require either trimming the legs of the stool or purchasing a commercially adjustable stool.

acher Elements of reading music are first introduced on student book page 4. Have students say or sing the letter names of the pitches, as well as say "rest" during the quarter rests. Note names appear inside each note on exercises 1–9 to help beginners recognize note names and their location on the staff.

Beat = The *Pulse* of Music

The **beat** in music should be very steady, just like your pulse.

Quarter Note

♩ = 1 Beat of Sound

Notes tell us how high or low to play, and how long to play.

Quarter Rest

𝄽 = 1 Beat of Silence

Rests tell us to count silent beats.

Music Staff

The **music staff** has 5 lines and 4 spaces.

Bar Lines

Bar lines divide the music staff into **measures**.

Measures

The **measures** on this page have four beats each.

THEORY

Measure   Measure

Music Staff

Bar Line   Bar Line   Bar Line

acher If you are going to use the *Essential Elements 2000 for Strings* accompanying CD in class begin by playing track one: Tuning Track. Compare and tune each of the student's instruments open strings to the CD. To save time tune only those strings that will be played in class that day. Instruct students to wait quietly while you tune the instruments. As students' playing skills develop, begin teaching them how to tune their own strings using the fine tune tuners or machine-head pegs on their instruments.

Demonstrate to students how to pluck their open strings, either in guitar or shoulder position. For violins and violas it is easier to pluck with the right thumb when holding the instrument in guitar position; in shoulder position it is easiest for students to use their right index finger.

Have students say and spell pizzicato. Point out to students the abbreviation *pizz.* for pizzicato.

acher All musical selections in *Essential Elements 2000 for Strings* are accompanied on the Play-Along CD recordings, available on CD from your local music dealer. Recorded accompaniments for the first 71 exercises are included on the CD enclosed in the student books and the Teacher's Manual. Professional musicians on acoustic instruments perform the recordings. Students may play with the recordings, as they are designed to guide and encourage students' home practice and enliven class rehearsal. Recordings provide a harmonic background for each selection and a performance model for students to emulate. Research strongly suggests that modeling and harmonic accompaniment promotes students' development of intonation.

Play-Along recording accompaniments are recorded at tempos playable by beginning students and include diverse styles of music, including rock, country, and classical. Use of recordings in class frees the string teacher to move throughout the class and assist individual student playing. Please note that the *Essential Elements 2000 for Strings* piano accompaniments are easier to play than those on the recordings so that you may focus on your students' performance, not your keyboard skills.

. TUNING TRACK *Wait quietly for your teacher to tune your instrument.*

acher Remind violin and viola students to keep their bows in their cases. Request cello and bass students to take the bow out of their case first before removing the instrument. They may place the bow on the floor by their chair or stool, or on their music stand. Students will begin developing bowing skills on student book page 7.

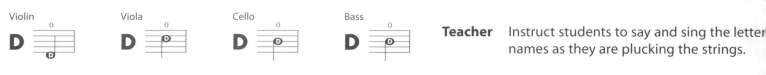

Teacher   Instruct students to say and sing the letter names as they are plucking the strings.

2. LET'S PLAY "OPEN D"

Piano accompaniments have been arranged to match the style and harmony of the accompaniments heard on the play-along CD.

3. LET'S PLAY "OPEN A"

TWO'S A TEAM

AT PIERROT'S DOOR   *The melody is on your CD.*

Teacher Once students can pizzicato the open strings in exercise 5 you may either play the melody on your string instrument while the students are plucking, or play the CD which features the melody on track 5.

Teacher Read the definitions of clef, time signature, and double bar that appear on student book page 5. Point out the note names as they appear in different clefs. Have students point to the time signatures and double bars on the page.

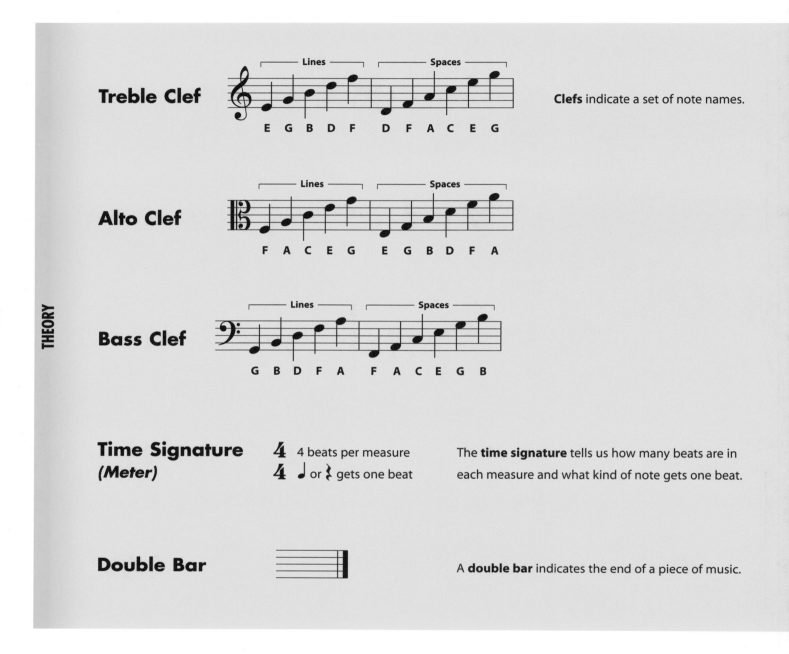

Treble Clef

Lines — Spaces

E G B D F   D F A C E G

Clefs indicate a set of note names.

Alto Clef

Lines — Spaces

F A C E G   E G B D F A

Bass Clef

Lines — Spaces

G B D F A   F A C E G B

Time Signature
(Meter)

4 beats per measure

♩ or 𝄽 gets one beat

The **time signature** tells us how many beats are in each measure and what kind of note gets one beat.

Double Bar

A **double bar** indicates the end of a piece of music.

THEORY

JUMPING JACKS *Identify the clef and time signature before playing.*

Teacher   Read the definition of repeat sign and note the symbol. Point out the repeat sign in exercise 8.

Demonstrate your preferred method of counting, clapping and tapping. This book uses a traditional counting system and teaches the subdivided beat from the beginning. If you elect to use another counting system, have students write the syllables or system in their books, including subdivided beats.

Counting is shown below the staff in each student book. We strongly encourage you to count, sing, and clap all exercises with your students before playing them. A counting system is not shown below all exercises, so that students will develop rhythmic and counting independence.

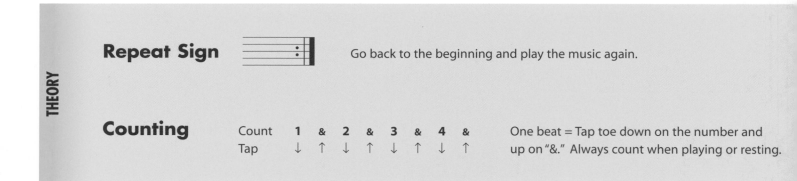

THEORY

Repeat Sign   Go back to the beginning and play the music again.

Counting   Count   **1   &   2   &   3   &   4   &**   One beat = Tap toe down on the number and
                 Tap   ↓   ↑   ↓   ↑   ↓   ↑   ↓   ↑   up on "&." Always count when playing or resting.

8. COUNT CAREFULLY   *Keep a steady beat when playing or resting.*

Student books have repeats,
not 1st and 2nd endings (until ex. 76).

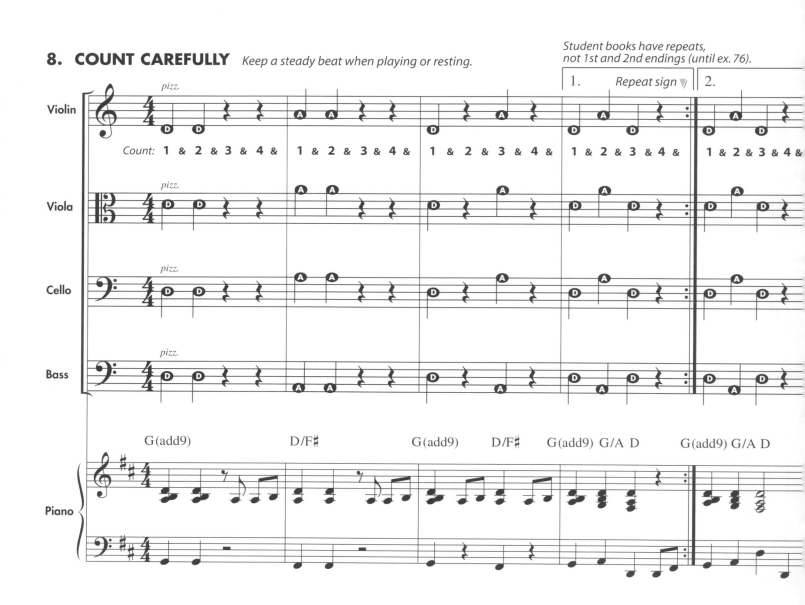

eacher Performance objectives of each quiz are listed. Objectives highlight the exact elements being reviewed and tested. Review exercises suggest specific examples for students requiring additional practice. Be certain students meet your performance expectations on every quiz.

QUIZ OBJECTIVES
- Pizzicato D and A strings
- Counting quarter notes and rests using subdivided beats
- Steady beat

Review Exercises:
> 4. *Two's A Team*
> 6. *Jumping Jacks*
> 8. *Count Carefully*

eacher Have students write in the counting for exercise 9. Check to be sure they have written in both the number and subdivided "&" for each pulse.

9. ESSENTIAL ELEMENTS QUIZ
Write in the counting before you play.

Student books have repeats, not 1st and 2nd endings (until ex. 76).

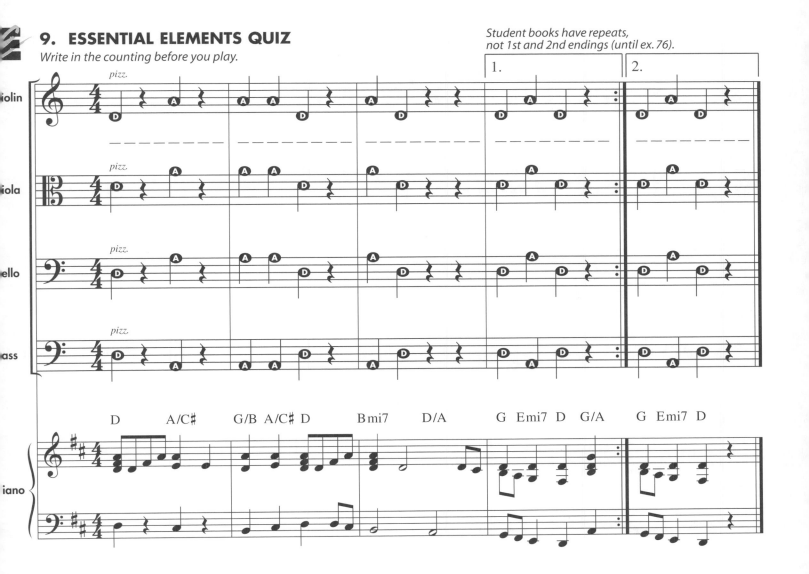

Teacher In string teaching, beginning players first put the sounding finger and all lower numbered fingers on the string together to play a pitch. This is called block fingering. After students' left hand shapes are well established they may begin to use independent fingering, placing only the sounding finger on the string for a pitch.

To help students develop their left-hand shape, the first notes introduced use three fingers for violin/viola and fou fingers for cello. Basses should place four fingers on the D string for the pitch F sharp while sounding their open G string when beginning to play. In addition to helping students shape their left hand, playing pitches first that use many fingers is better for students because it is easier to lift off fingers than add them. This approach also he students establish better intonation.

Have students hold up their left hand and position their fingers as in the drawing on student book page 6. Point out to violin and viola students the second and third fingers touch. Have students say the finger numbers out lou Notice that the thumb is not a numbered finger in string playing.

Violin/ To help students properly shape their left hand, their index finger should form a square. The square is formed by
Viola the fingernail, top of the finger, side of the finger, and the fingerboard. The side of the index finger should touch be near the side of the fingerboard near the base hand knuckle. This allows the other fingers to be poised over th fingerboard for better playing and intonation, and promotes a straight and relaxed left wrist. Failure to form this square first finger prevents students from properly developing all other left hand skills.

Also notice that the thumb is positioned on the side and is across from the first fingertip. Have students gently ta their thumb on the side of the fingerboard near the first fingertip to find the most natural position of the thumb.

Notice that the player's fingernails are short so that the fingers may be positioned on their tips. Point out to stud how the left arm and hand are in a straight line. The wrist should be generally straight, though relaxed.

Violin

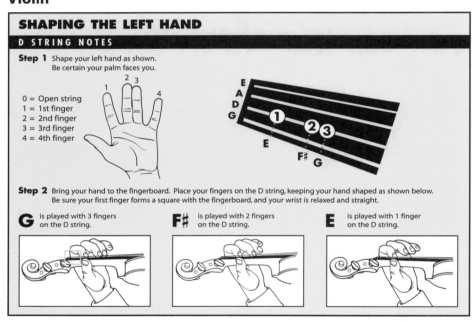

Viola

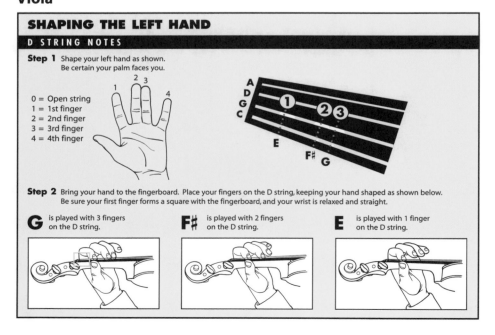

Cello

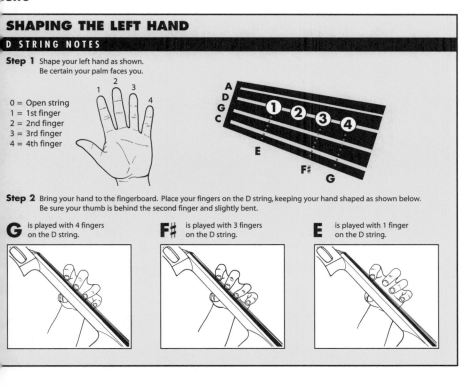

SHAPING THE LEFT HAND

D STRING NOTES

Step 1 Shape your left hand as shown. Be certain your palm faces you.

0 = Open string
1 = 1st finger
2 = 2nd finger
3 = 3rd finger
4 = 4th finger

Step 2 Bring your hand to the fingerboard. Place your fingers on the D string, keeping your hand shaped as shown below. Be sure your thumb is behind the second finger and slightly bent.

G is played with 4 fingers on the D string.

F♯ is played with 3 fingers on the D string.

E is played with 1 finger on the D string.

Bass

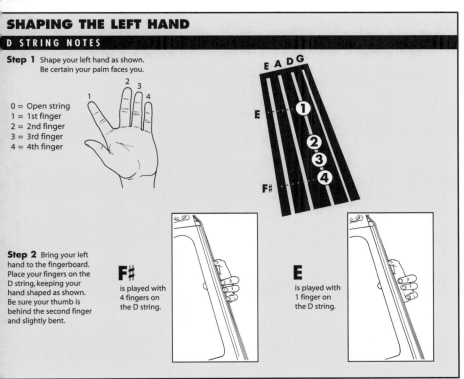

SHAPING THE LEFT HAND

D STRING NOTES

Step 1 Shape your left hand as shown. Be certain your palm faces you.

0 = Open string
1 = 1st finger
2 = 2nd finger
3 = 3rd finger
4 = 4th finger

Step 2 Bring your left hand to the fingerboard. Place your fingers on the D string, keeping your hand shaped as shown. Be sure your thumb is behind the second finger and slightly bent.

F♯ is played with 4 fingers on the D string.

E is played with 1 finger on the D string.

Teacher Checkpoints Teachers are encouraged to develop checkpoints for quickly evaluating students' playing skills. A list of checkpoints for student skills introduced on student book page 6 would include:

- Body position
- Feet position
- Instrument position
- Fingers curved over strings
- Thumb shape and position
- Violin/Viola: square first finger
- Left wrist straight and relaxed

Listening Skills   Play what your teacher plays. Listen carefully.

Teacher   Listening Skills are included every time a new note is introduced. Research suggests that students with well-developed listening skills have better left/right hand coordination, intonation, sound production, and memorization skills.

Teachers are given sample four-beat patterns for students to echo. The echo patterns may be played on any instrument and should be played behind the class so that students cannot see the teacher's fingering. These echo patterns are in treble clef and are only suggestions. Teachers are encouraged to create their own echo patterns. In the beginning, teachers may play echo patterns either pizzicato or with the bow for students to imitate.

Teacher   All finger numbers for pitches appear above the printed notes, and counting symbols below. Each time a new note is introduced, the rhythm in all the exercises immediately following is the same. This allows students to learn one new skill at a time.

Saying letter names out loud, singing letter names, or using solfeggio syllables before and/or during each exercise helps students develop pitch recognition, note reading, and accurate intonation.

As students begin to pizzicato their first left-hand pitches, instruct them to pizzicato quietly, so their left hand will remain relaxed on the fingerboard. Players only need enough weight on the string with their left hand to sound the pitch. No excessive weight or squeezing is needed.

10. LET'S READ "G"   *Start memorizing the note names.*

Teacher   In the first part of this method, sharp is being used as an accidental, not as a part of the key signature.

Sharp	♯	A **sharp** raises the sound of notes and remains in effect for the entire measure. Notes without sharps are called **natural** notes.

11. LET'S READ "F♯" (F-sharp)

Teacher Beginning in exercise 12 the letter name in a repeated note head occurs only in the first pitch. Students should be encouraged to recognize the name of those notes without the alphabet letters as they are note reading and playing.

Encourage students to keep their fingers near the string when lifting off the strings in exercise 12. The fingers that are not on the string should be curved over the strings. The line underneath the staff in the bass part is a bracket indicating that students should keep fingers down while playing additional pitches. This promotes proper left hand shape and intonation. Also, check that violin and viola students are consistently maintaining a square first finger shape as they are playing.

As students are playing the exercises on page 6, encourage them to compare their left hand shape with the drawings.

2. LIFT OFF

Student Is your left hand shaped as shown in the diagrams above?

Teacher The line underneath the staff in exercise 12 in the bass is a bracket indicating that students should keep fingers down while playing additional pitches. This promotes proper left hand shape and intonation. Once students consistently demonstrate an acceptable left-hand shape they may begin to use independent fingering-playing a pitch with only one finger on the string.

Teacher   BOW BUILDER ONE appears at the top of student book page 7. The purpose of BOW BUILDERS is to present activities for students to develop their bowing skills independent of their left-hand skills. Students should practice the BOW BUILDER exercises frequently until they are mastered.

The purpose of BOW BUILDER ONE: PENCIL HOLD is to help students develop a well shaped bow hand position. Shaping the bow hand on a pencil first allows students to focus on the hand shape without having to hold the bow.

Each of the five steps in BOW BUILDER ONE should be practiced daily until the skills are mastered. It is critically important for students to master forming their bow hand shape. The successful combination of bowing with instrument position and left hand skills introduced on student book page 18 depends on how well students master each of the BOW BUILDERS in this book.

Violin

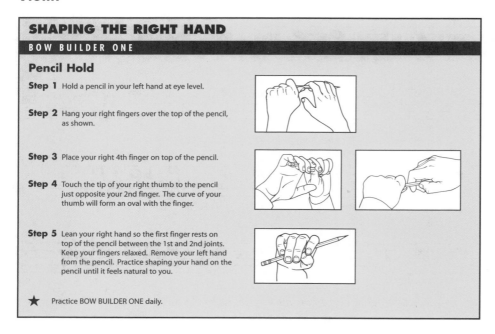

SHAPING THE RIGHT HAND

BOW BUILDER ONE

Pencil Hold

Step 1   Hold a pencil in your left hand at eye level.

Step 2   Hang your right fingers over the top of the pencil, as shown.

Step 3   Place your right 4th finger on top of the pencil.

Step 4   Touch the tip of your right thumb to the pencil just opposite your 2nd finger. The curve of your thumb will form an oval with the finger.

Step 5   Lean your right hand so the first finger rests on top of the pencil between the 1st and 2nd joints. Keep your fingers relaxed. Remove your left hand from the pencil. Practice shaping your hand on the pencil until it feels natural to you.

★   Practice BOW BUILDER ONE daily.

Viola

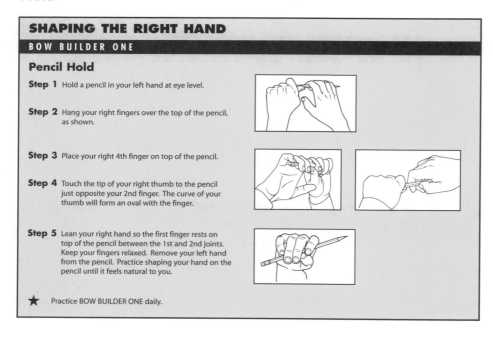

SHAPING THE RIGHT HAND

BOW BUILDER ONE

Pencil Hold

Step 1   Hold a pencil in your left hand at eye level.

Step 2   Hang your right fingers over the top of the pencil, as shown.

Step 3   Place your right 4th finger on top of the pencil.

Step 4   Touch the tip of your right thumb to the pencil just opposite your 2nd finger. The curve of your thumb will form an oval with the finger.

Step 5   Lean your right hand so the first finger rests on top of the pencil between the 1st and 2nd joints. Keep your fingers relaxed. Remove your left hand from the pencil. Practice shaping your hand on the pencil until it feels natural to you.

★   Practice BOW BUILDER ONE daily.

Cello

SHAPING THE RIGHT HAND
BOW BUILDER ONE

Pencil Hold

Step 1 Hold a pencil in your left hand about waist level.

Step 2 Place the tip of your right thumb between the first and second joints of your second finger.

Step 3 Place the pencil between your thumb and second finger, while keeping your thumb gently curved.

Step 4 The pencil should touch your first three fingers between the first and second joints, and touch the fourth finger at the first joint, as shown.

Step 5 Remove your left hand from the pencil. Keep your fingers relaxed. Practice shaping your hand on the pencil until it feels natural to you.

★ Practice BOW BUILDER ONE daily.

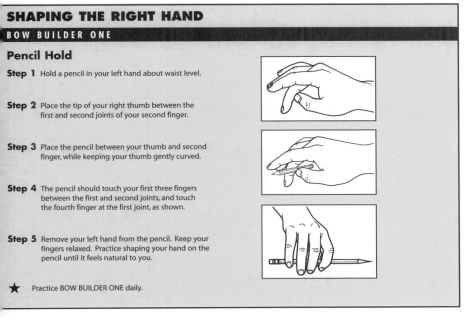

Bass

SHAPING THE RIGHT HAND
BOW BUILDER ONE

Pencil Hold

Step 1 Hold a pencil in your left hand about waist level.

Step 2 Place the tip of your right thumb between the first and second joints of your second finger.

Step 3 Place the pencil between your thumb and second finger, while keeping your thumb gently curved.

Step 4 The pencil should touch your first three fingers between the first and second joints, and touch the fourth finger at the first joint, as shown.

Step 5 Remove your left hand from the pencil. Keep your fingers relaxed. Practice shaping your hand on the pencil until it feels natural to you.

★ Practice BOW BUILDER ONE daily.

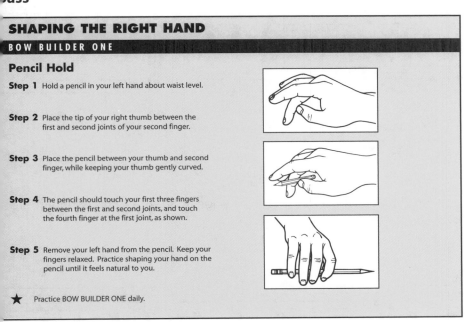

Violin/ Viola

The following illustrations show acceptable and unacceptable left hand positions. Note the placement of the thumb. Note in acceptable position the thumb is on its side slightly and positioned near the first fingertip. One successful teaching strategy to help students develop an acceptable left hand position is to have them slide their thumb forward as illustrated, promoting a better left hand shape and a straight, but relaxed, wrist position.

Unacceptable

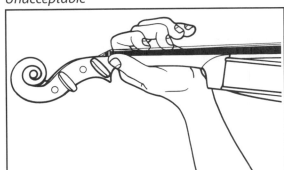

Acceptable

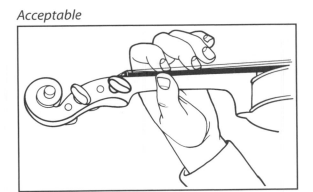

Teacher   It is recommended that as students learn to play each new pitch that they also memorize the letter name of each note. Spend time in class reviewing note names as students learn to play new pitches.

13. ON THE TRAIL *Say or sing the note names before you play.*

Violin/   Remind students to carefully form a square first finger shape as illustrated on page 6. Be sure all other fingers are
Viola   poised over the string for all instruments.

14. LET'S READ "E"

eacher   Be sure students review their counting, including subdivisions, when playing exercise 15.

5. WALKING SONG

Student books have repeats, not 1st and 2nd endings (until ex. 76).

QUIZ OBJECTIVES – ICE DANCING

- Pizzicato notes on D string (pizzicato G string on Bass)
- Counting
- Steady beat
- Square first finger shape (Violin/Viola)
- Recognizing, writing, and reading clef signs, time signatures, and double bar lines

Review Exercises:

13. *On the Trail*
14. *Let's Read "E"*
15. *Walking Song*

- Have students write the clef sign for their instrument
- Have students write $\frac{4}{4}$ time signatures

16. ESSENTIAL ELEMENTS QUIZ

Draw the missing symbols where they belong before you play:

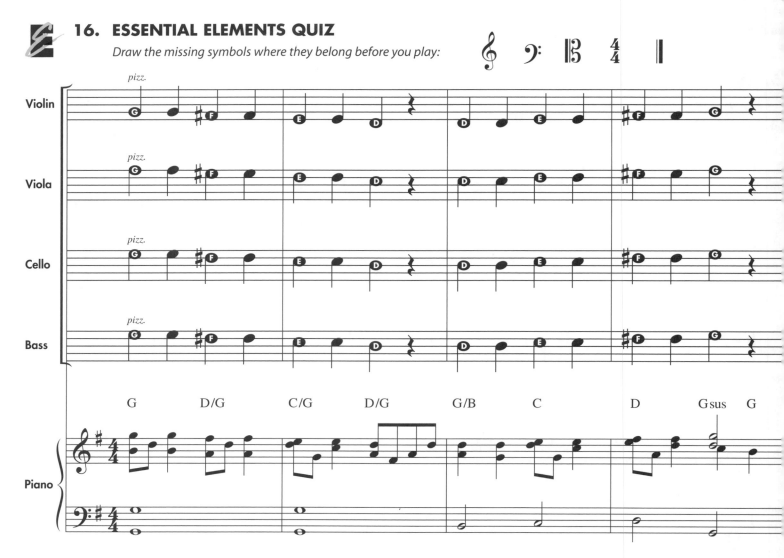

Teacher   BOW BUILDER TWO and BOW BUILDER THREE are introduced at the top of student book page 8. Have students master BOW BUILDER TWO before proceeding to BOW BUILDER THREE. BOW BUILDER TWO: PENCIL HOLD EXERCISES will help students develop curved, relaxed, flexible fingers and thumbs. BOW BUILDER THREE: BOWING MOTIONS will help students develop proper violin/viola bowing motion from the elbow, not the shoulder. *Elbow Energy* develops cello students bowing skills, as does *The Pendulum* for basses.

Violin/Viola

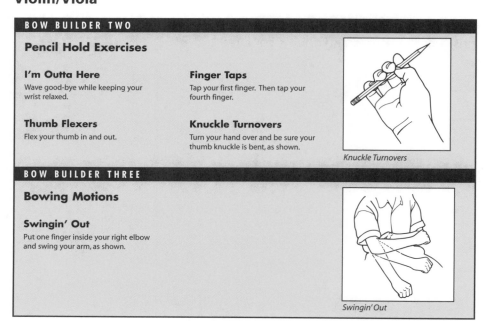

BOW BUILDER TWO

Pencil Hold Exercises

I'm Outta Here
Wave good-bye while keeping your wrist relaxed.

Thumb Flexers
Flex your thumb in and out.

Finger Taps
Tap your first finger. Then tap your fourth finger.

Knuckle Turnovers
Turn your hand over and be sure your thumb knuckle is bent, as shown.

Knuckle Turnovers

BOW BUILDER THREE

Bowing Motions

Swingin' Out
Put one finger inside your right elbow and swing your arm, as shown.

Swingin' Out

Cello

BOW BUILDER TWO

Pencil Hold Exercises

I'm Outta Here
Wave good-bye while keeping your wrist relaxed.

Thumb Flexers
Flex your thumb in and out.

Finger Taps
Tap your first finger. Then tap your fourth finger.

Knuckle Turnovers
Turn your hand over and be sure your thumb knuckle is bent, as shown.

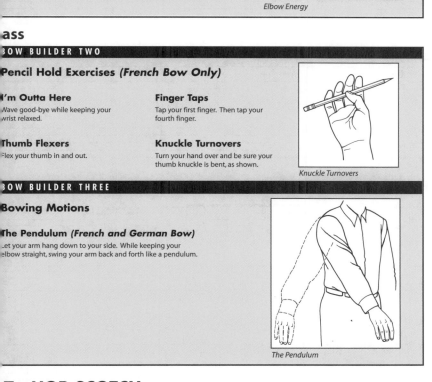

Knuckle Turnovers

BOW BUILDER THREE

Bowing Motions

Elbow Energy
- Swing your right elbow away from your body.
- Open your right forearm, as shown.
- Close your right forearm.
- Swing your elbow back toward your body.

Elbow Energy

Bass

BOW BUILDER TWO

Pencil Hold Exercises *(French Bow Only)*

I'm Outta Here
Wave good-bye while keeping your wrist relaxed.

Thumb Flexers
Flex your thumb in and out.

Finger Taps
Tap your first finger. Then tap your fourth finger.

Knuckle Turnovers
Turn your hand over and be sure your thumb knuckle is bent, as shown.

Knuckle Turnovers

BOW BUILDER THREE

Bowing Motions

The Pendulum *(French and German Bow)*
Let your arm hang down to your side. While keeping your elbow straight, swing your arm back and forth like a pendulum.

The Pendulum

7. HOP SCOTCH

Folk songs have been an important part of cultures for centuries and have been passed on from generation to generation. Folk song melodies help define the sound of a culture or region. This folk song comes from the Slavic region of eastern Europe.

Teacher   Familiarize students with different types of folk music by playing recorded examples of Slavic folk music. Discuss examples of American folk music, e.g. *Skip To My Lou, Long Long Ago.*

18. MORNING DANCE

Slavic Folk Song

Student books have repeats,
not 1st and 2nd endings (until ex. 76).

9. ROLLING ALONG

Go to next line. ▼

**Violin/
Viola**   Review holding the violin or viola in shoulder position as shown on page 3. Check to see if the scroll is generally parallel to the floor and positioned over the left foot. Also check the location of the instrument button. It should be either near or touching the middle of the neck, with the side corner of the jaw resting on the chin rest and the head erect.

**Violin/
Viola/
Cello**   The following *Workouts* will help your students develop a relaxed left hand. Violin/Viola students should now be spending more time playing in shoulder position than in guitar position. Left-hand exercises were not included in the student bass book because of the space devoted to the two different bow holds: French and German. However, bass students can do these exercises also.

Practice each of the *Workout* exercises with students until they have mastered them. The foundation for more advanced left-hand skills is being established by successfully mastering each of the *Workouts*. Demonstrate each of the *Workouts* for the students before they practice them.

Violin

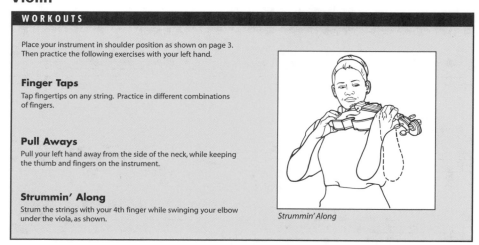

WORKOUTS

Place your instrument in shoulder position as shown on page 3. Then practice the following exercises with your left hand.

Finger Taps

Tap fingertips on any string. Practice in different combinations of fingers.

Pull Aways

Pull your left hand away from the side of the neck, while keeping the thumb and fingers on the instrument.

Strummin' Along

Strum the strings with your 4th finger while swinging your elbow under the viola, as shown.

Strummin' Along

Viola

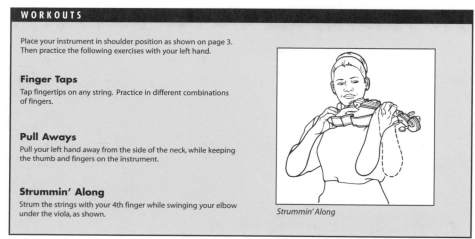

WORKOUTS

Place your instrument in shoulder position as shown on page 3. Then practice the following exercises with your left hand.

Finger Taps

Tap fingertips on any string. Practice in different combinations of fingers.

Pull Aways

Pull your left hand away from the side of the neck, while keeping the thumb and fingers on the instrument.

Strummin' Along

Strum the strings with your 4th finger while swinging your elbow under the viola, as shown.

Strummin' Along

Cello

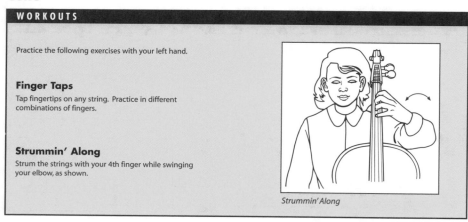

WORKOUTS

Practice the following exercises with your left hand.

Finger Taps

Tap fingertips on any string. Practice in different combinations of fingers.

Strummin' Along

Strum the strings with your 4th finger while swinging your elbow, as shown.

Strummin' Along

Bass

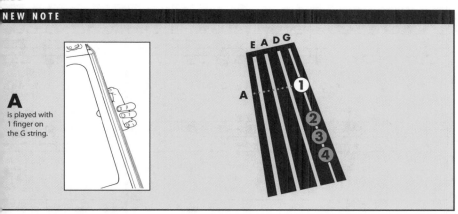

NEW NOTE

A is played with 1 finger on the G string.

Bass

Bass

The note A played in first position on the double bass is introduced in exercise 20. There are no new notes introduced in the violin, viola, or cello student books. Those instruments are playing their open A string while the bass is fingering the A on the G string.

In exercise 20, *Good King Wenceslas,* for the first time the violin, viola, and cello students should keep their fingers down on some pitches while playing others. Basses did this first in exercise 12. This helps students develop a well-shaped left-hand position when first learning to play.

The words to *Good King Wenceslas* are provided on page 260. Have students say and sing the words to *Good King Wenceslas* as they are learning to play the melody.

20. GOOD KING WENCESLAS

Welsh Folk Song

Student books have repeats, not 1st and 2nd endings (until ex. 76).

21. SEMINOLE CHANT

Student books have repeats,
not 1st and 2nd endings (until ex. 76).

QUIZ OBJECTIVES – LIGHTLY ROW

- Pizzicato notes on D string (and the G string on Bass)
- Counting
- Steady beat
- Square first finger shape (Violin/Viola)
- Keeping fingers down while playing pitches on another string
- Violin and Viola shoulder position

Review Exercises:

Page 9 *Workouts*

19. *Rolling Along*

20. *Seminole Chant*

21. *Good King Wenceslas*

The words to *Lightly Row* are provided on page 260. Have students say and sing the words as they prepare to play *Lightly Row*.

22. ESSENTIAL ELEMENTS QUIZ – LIGHTLY ROW

△ *Prepare F♯ before playing (except Bass).*

Teacher   The pitches D, C♯, and B are introduced. D and C♯ notes are in third position on the double bass so that bass students will be able to avoid octave displacements. Research suggests that students have difficulty recognizing and understanding a melodic line that contains octave displacements. Point out to bass students that their finger spacing in third position is the same as in first position, and that the thumb remains behind the second finger.

For developing student listening skills sample four-beat patterns are provided that incorporate the new pitches introduced on student book page 10. Play the pitch patterns provided, or ones you create, for students to echo so that they may continue to develop their listening skills. Remember the echo patterns may be played on any instrument and should be played behind the class so that students cannot see the teacher's fingering.

Remind students to memorize the names of the new notes they are learning to play.

Violin/Viola

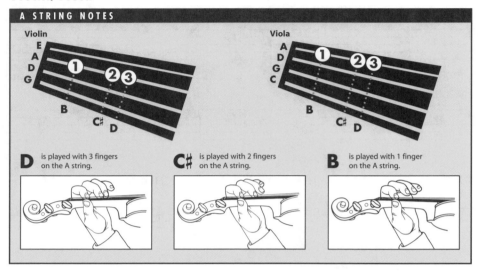

Cello

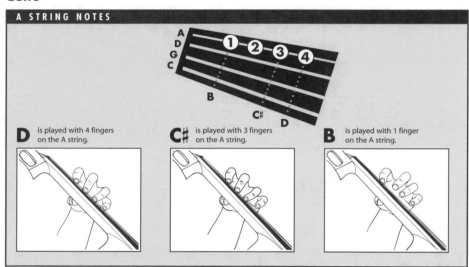

Bass

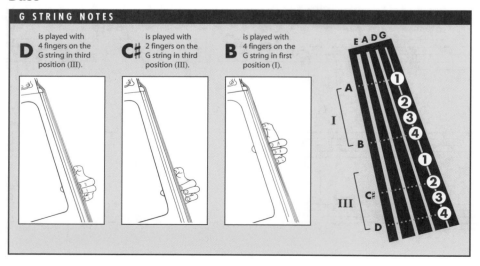

Listening Skills

Play what your teacher plays. Listen carefully.

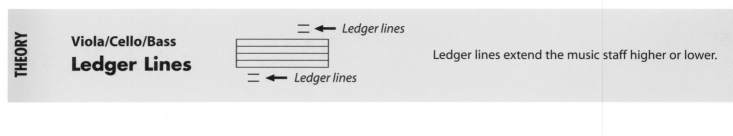

THEORY

Viola/Cello/Bass
Ledger Lines

Ledger lines extend the music staff higher or lower.

Violin   Viola   Cello   Bass

23. LET'S READ "D"

24. LET'S READ "C#" (C-sharp)

Play all C#'s. Sharps apply to the entire measure.

25. TAKE OFF

26. CARIBBEAN ISLAND

*Student books have repeats,
not 1st and 2nd endings (until ex. 76).*

Student ⭐ Practice BOW BUILDERS ONE, TWO, and THREE daily.

Teacher Continually review the counting system you have selected with students as they learn to play each exercise. It is recommended that students count aloud each exercise while they are playing. Review BOW BUILDERS ONE, TWO, and THREE daily with students until they are mastered..

Teacher Have students compare their fingered D to the open D string in measures 1, 4 of exercise 27, *Olympic High Jump.* Point out to students that both pitches are D, only an octave apart. Ask students to find another D on their instrument by moving their left hand along the fingerboard, using their ear to guide them.

27. OLYMPIC HIGH JUMP

Teacher   Students learn a new note, B, in exercise 28. Remind students to memorize the note name as they are learning to play the note.

28.   LET'S READ "B"

In exercise 29, *Half Way Down,* basses shift for the first time. They shift from third to first position in measure 3 to play B. Instruct basses to release their hand weight on the string before and during the shift and that the thumb and hand move together as a unit. The thumb should remain by the second finger. Students may practice the shifting motion in the air away from the bass to help develop their shifting skill. Bass students should also practice shifting back and forth from C# to B and from B to C# in preparation for exercise 30, *Right Back Up.*

Dashes before finger numbers are used to indicate both ascending and descending shifts. Four positions are used in Book I and are indicated in students books by Roman Numerals:

I = First position (first finger plays A on the G string)

II = Second position (first finger plays B♭ on the G string)

III = Third position (first finger plays C on the G string)

Bass
Shifting
Sliding your left hand smoothly and lightly to a new location on the fingerboard, indicated by a dash (–).

9. HALF WAY DOWN

Bass   Basses shift from first to third position.

30. RIGHT BACK UP

Teacher   Read the definition of scales. Demonstrate examples of various scales. Point out that scales begin and end on the same note.

Ashbf A descending scale is introduced first because it helps promote the left-hand shape of the violins, violas, and cellos. Also, it is easier for students to lift off fingers while maintaining an acceptable left-hand shape as they are playing a descending scale.

Reviewing the names of the notes with students is an excellent activity while students are practicing their D major scale on student book page 11.

THEORY

Scale   A **scale** is a sequence of notes in ascending or descending order. Like a musical "ladder", each note is the next consecutive step of the scale. This is your D Scale. The first and last notes are both D.

1. DOWN THE D SCALE *Remember to memorize the note names.*

QUIZ OBJECTIVES – UP THE D SCALE

- Left-hand shape
- Bass shifting
- Pizzicato D major scale

Review Exercises:

    29. *Half Way Down*
    30. *Right Back Up*

32. ESSENTIAL ELEMENTS QUIZ – UP THE D SCALE

eacher BOW BUILDER FOUR: ON THE BOW is introduced on the top of student book page 12. The purpose of this BOW BUILDER is to apply the hand shape previously positioned on a pen, pencil, or straw to the bow stick. Notice that the bow hand is positioned at the balance point of the bow for violin and viola. Students are able to hold the bow lightly if the hand is positioned first at the balance point. As students master the bow hand shape at the balance point they may begin to gradually move the hand to the frog.

The skills of holding the bow with an acceptable hand shape takes time for students to master. The authors recommend that students wait until their hand shape is mastered before setting the bow on the string to begin to learning bowing motions. While the bow hand is being mastered students may continue to work on their left hand, counting, listening, and note reading skills.

iolin/Viola

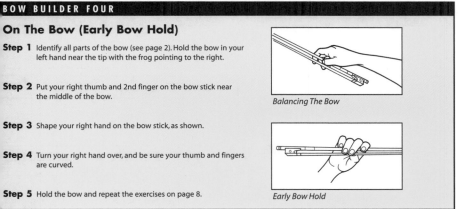

BOW BUILDER FOUR

On The Bow (Early Bow Hold)

Step 1 Identify all parts of the bow (see page 2). Hold the bow in your left hand near the tip with the frog pointing to the right.

Step 2 Put your right thumb and 2nd finger on the bow stick near the middle of the bow.

Step 3 Shape your right hand on the bow stick, as shown.

Step 4 Turn your right hand over, and be sure your thumb and fingers are curved.

Step 5 Hold the bow and repeat the exercises on page 8.

Balancing The Bow

Early Bow Hold

ello

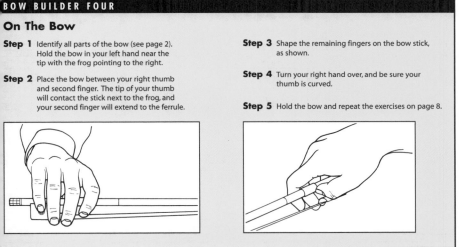

BOW BUILDER FOUR

On The Bow

Step 1 Identify all parts of the bow (see page 2). Hold the bow in your left hand near the tip with the frog pointing to the right.

Step 2 Place the bow between your right thumb and second finger. The tip of your thumb will contact the stick next to the frog, and your second finger will extend to the ferrule.

Step 3 Shape the remaining fingers on the bow stick, as shown.

Step 4 Turn your right hand over, and be sure your thumb is curved.

Step 5 Hold the bow and repeat the exercises on page 8.

ass

BOW BUILDER FOUR

On The Bow (French)

Step 1 Identify all parts of the bow (see page 2). Hold the bow in your left hand near the tip with the frog pointing to the right.

Step 2 Place the bow between your right thumb and second finger. The tip of your thumb will contact the stick next to the frog, and your second finger will extend to the ferrule.

Step 3 Shape the remaining fingers on the bow stick as shown.

Step 4 Turn your right hand over, and be sure your thumb is curved.

Step 5 Hold the bow and repeat the exercises on page 8.

On The Bow (German)

Step 1 Identify all parts of the bow (see page 2). Hold the bow in your left hand near the tip with the frog pointing to the right.

Step 2 Place the frog in your right hand at the base joints of your fingers.

Step 3 Put your thumb on top of the bow while the tips of the first and second fingers touch the side of the stick and frog.

Step 4 Hook your fourth finger underneath the frog touching the ferrule. Allow the third finger to curve and relax.

French Bow   *French Bow*   *German Bow*   *German Bow*

Alert   Do not place your bow on the instrument until instructed to do so by your teacher.

33. SONG FOR CHRISTINE

4. NATALIE'S ROSE *Remember to count.*

Teacher   The goal of exercise 35, *ESSENTIAL CREATIVITY*, is to reinforce students note reading skills in a creative manner. Students are asked to spell words using the pitches they have learned to play. Answers may include egg, bed, dad, fad, dog, cab, etc.

35. ESSENTIAL CREATIVITY   *How many words can you create by drawing notes on the staff below?*

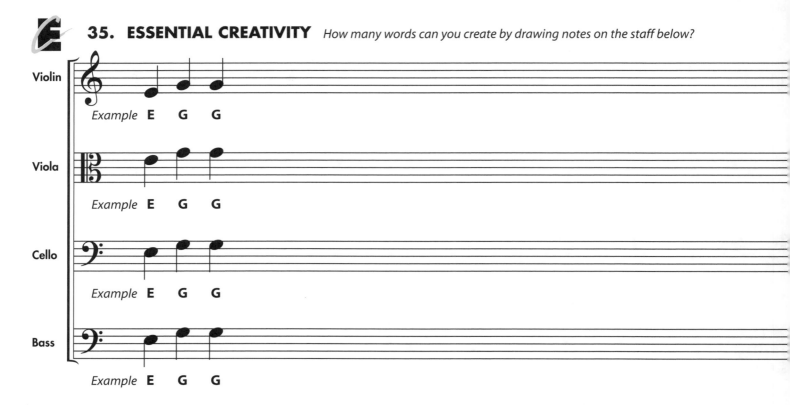

Teacher   The well-known folk song, *Dreidel,* is presented at the beginning of student book page 13. Familiarize students with other traditional Jewish folk songs by playing recorded examples in class. Discuss the history of Israel and its relationship to the United States.

Please note that *Dreidel* is the last exercise that includes alphabet letters in note heads to aid students in their note reading. Review students' note reading again, so that they will be successful in reading notes from this point on.

HISTORY   Folk songs often tell stories. This **Israeli folk song** describes a game played with a dreidel, a small table-top spinning toy that has been enjoyed by families for centuries. The game is especially popular in December around the time of Hanukkah.

36. DREIDEL

Israeli Folk Song

Teacher   The purpose of BOW BUILDER FIVE: SHADOW BOWING is to help students develop beginning bowing skills away from the instrument. This teaching strategy allows students to concentrate on only one skill at a time. The steps to begin teaching shadow bowing are the same for all four instruments.

Point out to students the definition of shadow bowing: bowing without the instrument. In BOW BUILDER FIVE, shadow bowing is done on rosin so that students will learn to pull the bow in a straight line. Shadow bowing may also be done by bowing in the air, through a PVC tube or paper product tube held in the air (cello/bass), or on the shoulder or arm (violin/viola).

First, demonstrate for students how to tighten and loosen the bow hair. Turn the screw of the bow clockwise to tighten, and counter-clockwise to loosen. Instruct students to always loosen the bow hair when they are finished playing.

Next, have students shadow bow on their rosin as illustrated on student book page 13. Basses should wait to use real bass rosin until page 16, or later, so that they can learn how to pull the bow in a straight line on a rectangular cake of rosin as illustrated.

Another way to practice shadow bowing is to bow through a PVC tube or paper product tube. Violin and viola students may hold the tube with their left hand over their left shoulder. They can place their bow inside the tube and bow through it to help learn their bowing motion. Cello and bass students may hold the tube in front of themselves where the bow would be contacting the string while bowing through the tube.

Review the definition and symbols for down and up bow. Demonstrate up and down bow directions for students.

Violin/Viola

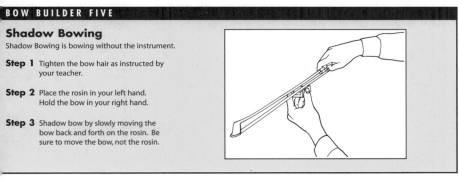

Cello

Bass

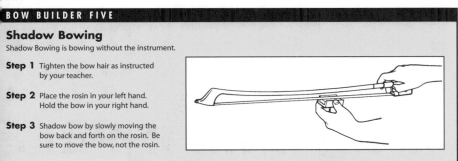

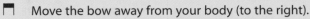

Down Bow   ⊓   Move the bow away from your body (to the right).

Up Bow   V   Move the bow toward your body (to the left).

Teacher   *Rosin Raps* 37–39 promote development of bowing skills away from the instrument so that students need to learn only one kinesthetic skill at a time. Rosin Raps also help students develop the physical coordination of reading music while bowing at the same time. Bowing on rosin is one way for students to shadow bow.

Have students say or sing "down" and "up" for bow direction and "rest" as indicated in the student book while bowing the following Rosin Raps. Have violin and viola students first bow the Rosin Raps with their bow hand positioned at the balance point. Once students can consistently bow the raps while keeping an acceptable bow-hand shape they may begin to gradually move their bow hand position to the frog.

As students are practicing the Rosin Raps encourage them to frequently compare their bow hand shape to the one in the illustration.

Student   Is your bow hand shaped as shown in the diagram above?

eacher Have students write the letter names of the notes in the theory exercise that appears at the top of student book page 14.

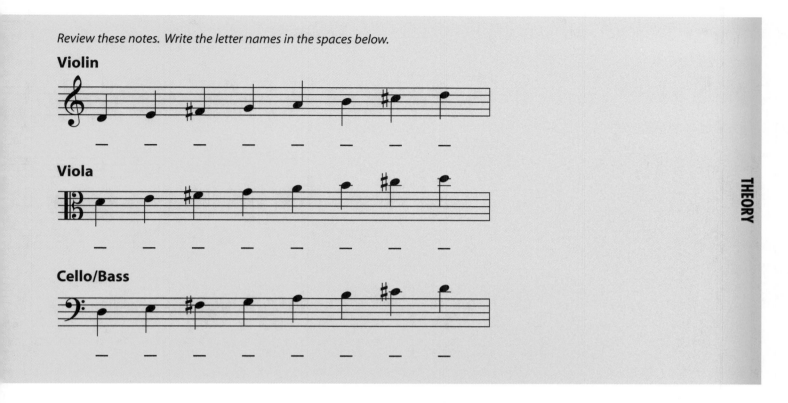

Review these notes. Write the letter names in the spaces below.

Violin

Viola

Cello/Bass

THEORY

eacher All remaining exercises will use regular music notation. Students should name the notes of the following examples to reinforce note reading skills.

While students are learning to pizzicato and read the note names in exercises 40–42 they should be continuing to practice BOW BUILDER FIVE in preparation for bowing on the string beginning on student book page 16.

0. CAROLINA BREEZE

41. JINGLE BELLS

J. S. Pierpont

42. OLD MACDONALD HAD A FARM

American Folk Song

Student ⭐ Practice BOW BUILDER FIVE daily.

HISTORY

Austrian composer **Wolfgang Amadeus Mozart** (1756–1791) was a child prodigy who first performed in concert at age 6. He lived during the time of the American Revolution (1775–1783). Mozart's music is melodic and imaginative. He wrote hundreds of compositions, including a piano piece based on this familiar song.

Teacher   Familiarize students with music of Mozart by playing recorded examples of his works. You may also want to use the movie Amadeus as a resource.

43. A MOZART MELODY

Adapted by W. A. Mozart

Key Signature: D MAJOR

THEORY

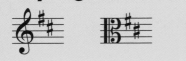

A **key signature** tells us what notes to play with sharps and flats throughout the entire piece. Play all F's as F# (F-sharp) and all C's as C# (C-sharp) when you see this key signature, which is called "D Major."

Teacher   Read the definition and example of key signature as presented on student book page 15. Give students examples of other key signatures and have them practice writing them. Be sure students are counting, including subdivisions when learning to play each exercise.

44. MATTHEW'S MARCH

45. CHRISTOPHER'S TUNE

Teacher   Have students create and write notes they choose to complete the melody in ESSENTIAL CREATIVITY, exercise 46. This allows students to begin composing their own melodies while reinforcing their note reading and rhythm reading skills. Give them the opportunity to play their completed melodies in class. Consider allowing students to play them on a concert.

46. ESSENTIAL CREATIVITY

Play the notes below. Then compose your own music for the last two measures using the notes you have learned with this rhythm:

Teacher BOW BUILDER SIX: LET'S BOW! is introduced at the top of student book page 16. The purpose of this exercise is to give students the opportunity to begin bowing on the string, using all the skills learned in the previous BOW BUILDERS.

Violin/Viola

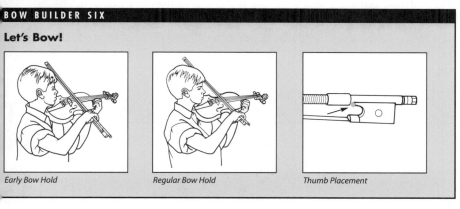

Early Bow Hold   *Regular Bow Hold*   *Thumb Placement*

Cello

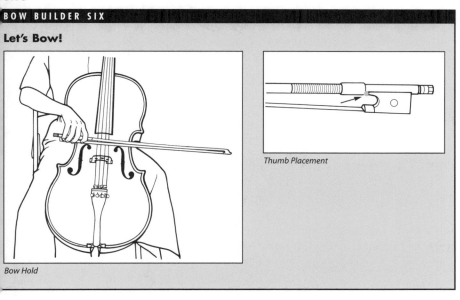

Thumb Placement

Bow Hold

Bass

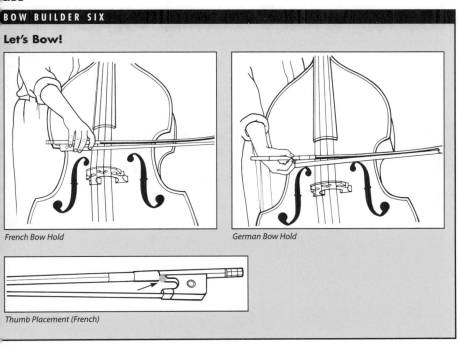

French Bow Hold   *German Bow Hold*

Thumb Placement (French)

**Violin/
Viola**   Even though students will only be bowing open strings first, be careful that they keep the proper shape and position of their left hand while bowing. Notice in the illustration that the left hand is on the bout where the neck and instrument meet and that all the fingers are curved. This finger position helps reinforce students left hand shape as they get ready to bow fingered notes.

Examine the illustration with a straw in the "F" hole. Notice that the straw is placed in the "F" hole near the low string of the student's instrument. The bow is placed between the bridge and the straw. The straw helps the student bow in a straight line parallel to the bridge. This bow placement will produce the best sound for students.

This illustration is in Teacher's Manual only.

Straw in the "F" hole

This illustration is in Teacher's Manual only.

Bowing through a tube

Teacher   Also notice the illustration with the bow traveling through a tube attached to the string. Bowing through a tube will help all string students learn the proper bowing motion. Either plastic PVC tubes or paper product tubes may be used. Place a rubber band under the strings and then loop the ends around each end of the tube.

Students should begin bowing with short bow strokes: violins and violas in the middle of the bow; cellos and basses in the lower half of the bow. As students' bowing skills develop, they should gradually lengthen their bow strokes.

Violin/Viola

Step 1   Hold the instrument with your left hand on the upper bout as illustrated.

Violin/Viola

Step 2   Hold the bow at the balance point (Early Bow Hold). Your right elbow should be slightly lower than your hand.

Your teacher will suggest when to begin moving your bow hand toward the frog, as shown in the Regular Bow Hold illustration. The tip of your thumb will move to the place on the stick where it touches the frog.

eacher   Model open D's and A's for students to echo. Evaluate the tone of students' echoes. The tone should be smooth, even, and pleasant to hear. Sample open string examples for echo practice with students are provided.

Listening Skills   Play what your teacher plays. Listen carefully.

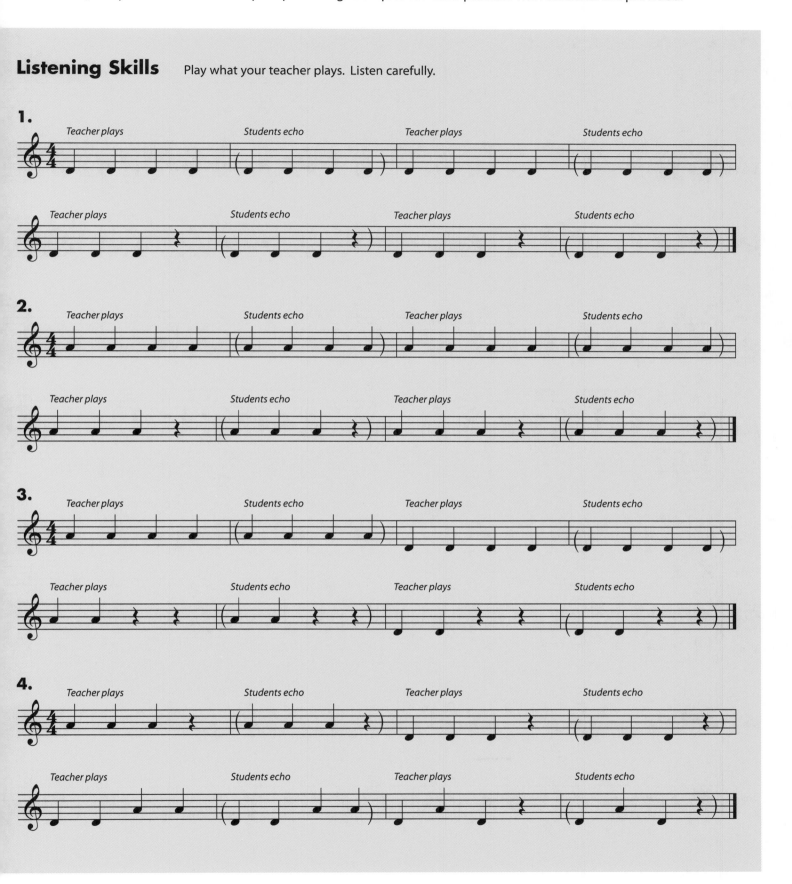

Teacher   As students develop their bowing skills, have them do some of the exercises on student book page 8 to relax their hand during the rests. For exercise 47, check to make sure that students' elbows are at the proper height when their bow is on the D string.

47. BOW ON THE D STRING

eacher Check to make sure that students' elbows are at the proper height for the A string.

8. BOW ON THE A STRING

Teacher   String levels, for string crossing motions, are introduced on student book page 17. Note that the motion to change string levels is the opposite for upper and lower strings, i.e., a player raises the right arm to play lower-pitched strings for violin/viola, but lowers the right arm to play lower-pitched strings on the cello/bass.

Be sure that students raise and lower their arms during the rests for each new string level in the following exercises.

Violin/Viola

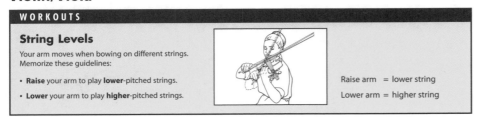

Cello

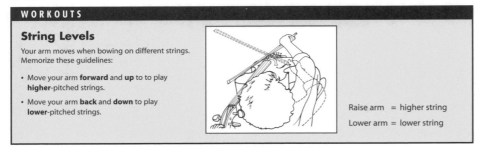

Bass

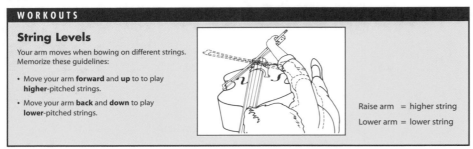

49. RAISE AND LOWER

Student books have a repeat sign in measure

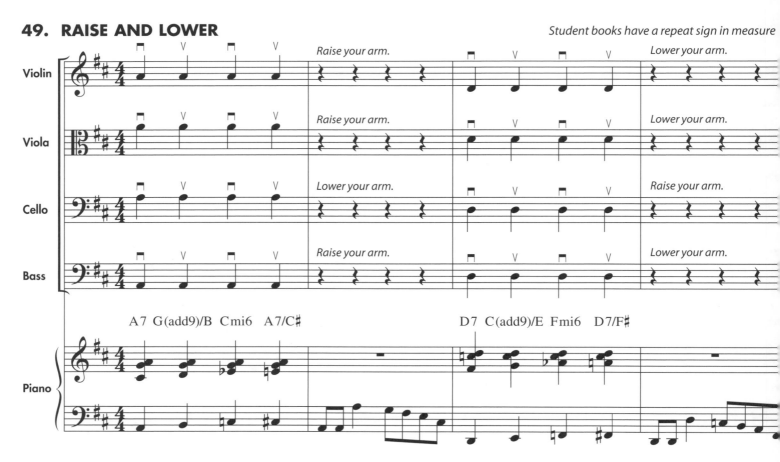

50. TEETER TOTTER

51. MIRROR IMAGE

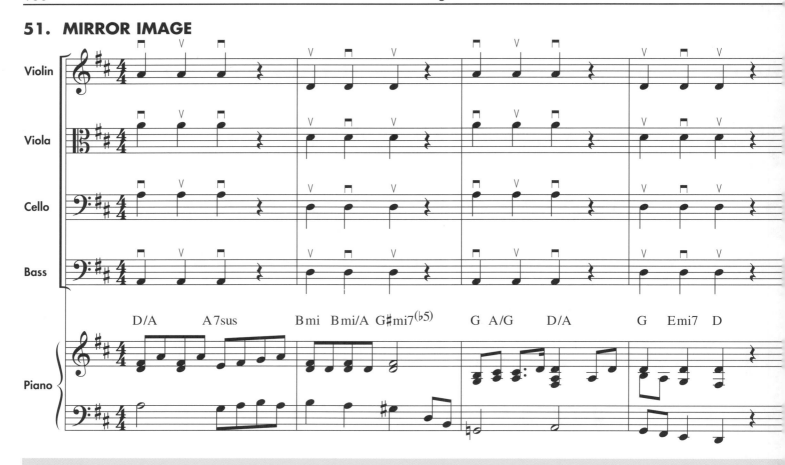

Bow Lift   ,   Lift the bow and return to its starting point.

Teacher   Read the definition and show students the symbol for bow lift. Practice lifting and setting the bow on the string with students. Be sure that students relax their shoulder, arm, wrist, and bow hand after they set the bow on the string each time before pulling the bow.

Be sure that students raise and lower their arms during the rests for each new string level in the following exercises. Notice that violin/viola and cello/bass levels are reversed.

52. A STRAND OF D 'N' A

QUIZ OBJECTIVES – OLYMPIC CHALLENGE
- Parallel bowing
- Smooth and even tone
- Arm level changes at string crossings

Review Exercises:
49. *Raise and Lower*
50. *Teeter Totter*
52. *A Strand of D'N'A*

53. ESSENTIAL ELEMENTS QUIZ – OLYMPIC CHALLENGE

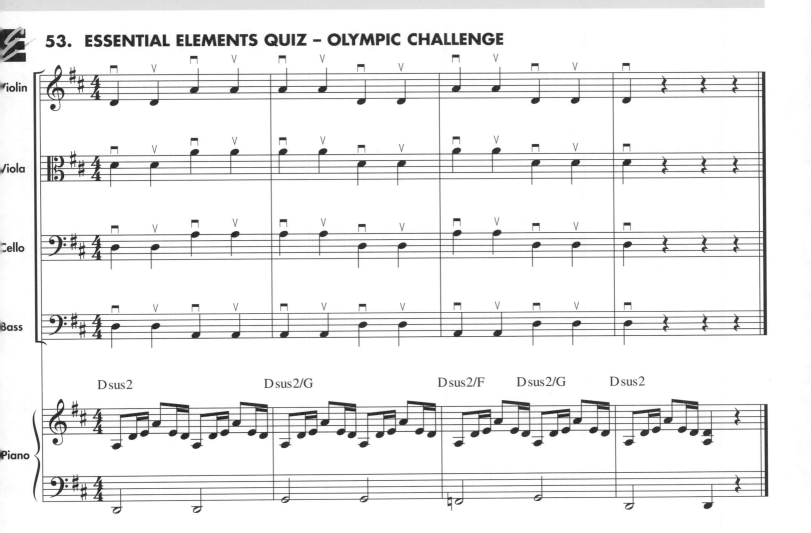

BOW BUILDER SEVEN

Combining Both Hands

Using notes from the D major scale, echo what your teacher plays.

Teacher   BOW BUILDER SEVEN: COMBINING BOTH HANDS involves the teacher playing pitch patterns and the students echoing those patterns. Before students proceed to page 18, be sure that they have mastered proper bow hand shape, beginning open string motions, and changing string level skills in the echo patterns. On page 18 students will begin to bow fingered notes for the first time. This is an important skill and students must first master bowing open string skills before they begin bowing fingered pitches.

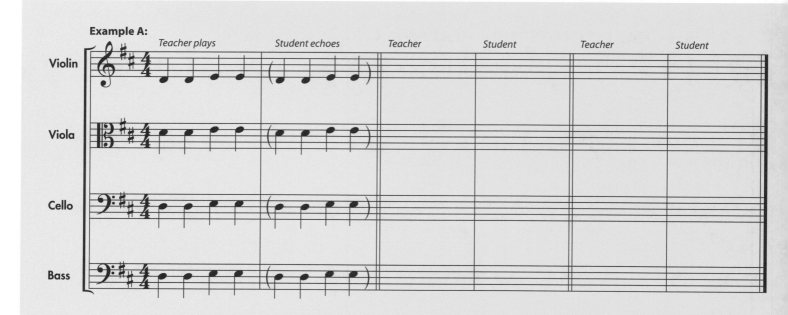

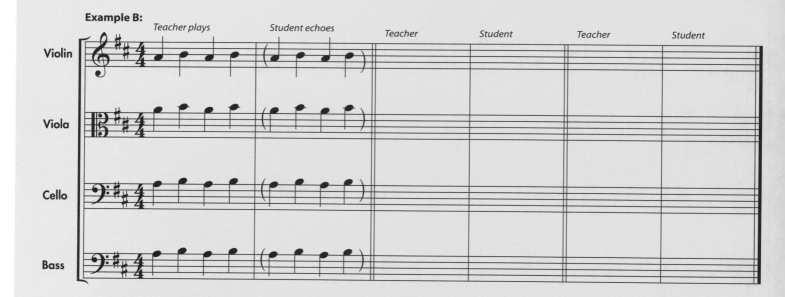

Teacher   Students should now be ready to begin learning to bow fingered pitches while reading music. A suggested practice routine is provided for them in the student text. These sequential practice steps are important for students to follow because they will help them develop successful playing skills and home practice skills. Lead students through these steps carefully for each of the remaining playing exercises, and encourage students to use these steps while practicing at home. Create and substitute additional practice steps as needed.

Remember, there are many different ways to shadow bow that can be used in Step 3, e.g. bowing in the air, bowing on rosin, or bowing through tubes attached to the instrument or held over the left shoulder (violin and viola) or in front (cello and bass). One way is to ask students to bow vertically in the air, being careful that the down bow motion is toward the floor and the up bow motion is toward the ceiling. Bowing vertically helps eliminate tension in the right hand, which will occur if the bow is held in the air horizontally while shadow bowing. Of course, you may always have students practice bowing their open strings.

PUTTING IT ALL TOGETHER

Congratulations! You are now ready to practice like an advanced player by combining left and right hand skills while reading music. When learning a new line of music, follow these steps for success:

Step 1   Tap your toe and say or sing the letter names.

Step 2   Play *pizz.* and say or sing the letter names.

Step 3   Shadow bow and say or sing the letter names.

Step 4   Bow and play as written.

54. BOWING "G"

55. BACK AND FORTH

56. DOWN AND UP

67. TRIBAL LAMENT

*Student books have repeats,
not 1st and 2nd endings (until ex. 76).*

8. BOWING "D"

59. LITTLE STEPS

60. ELEVATOR DOWN

eacher Counting and playing eighth notes will be introduced on student book page 20. Counting quarter note subdivisions was first introduced on page 5, with additional examples on successive pages. Give students further preparation for page 20 by counting aloud as a class, including subdivisions, for each of the exercises on page 19. The authors also recommend that students review their toe tapping skills as they play each exercise.

1. ELEVATOR UP

62. DOWN THE D MAJOR SCALE

3. SCALE SIMULATOR *Remember to count.*

QUIZ OBJECTIVES – THE D MAJOR SCALE
- Bowing and fingering D and A string notes
- Playing correct bow markings
- Bowing parallel to the bridge
- String Levels
- Half steps and whole steps

Review Exercises:
62. *Elevator Down*
63. *Down the D Scale*
63. *Scale Simulator*

Teacher   As students are practicing for exercise *64. Essential Elements Quiz – The D Major Scale,* encourage them to constantly evaluate their intonation. The half and whole steps must be in tune. Assisting students as they develop self-assessment skills is critical to developing effective practice skills.

64. ESSENTIAL ELEMENTS QUIZ – THE D MAJOR SCALE

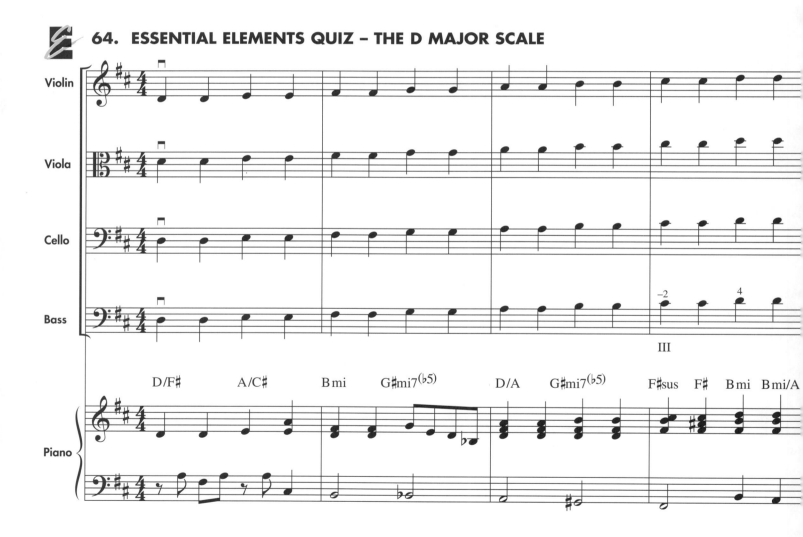

Teacher The basses learn the new note C♯ while the other instruments review note reading, bar lines, and counting through a written exercise.

Special Exercise (Violin/Viola/Cello)

While the basses learn a new note, draw the bar lines in the music below. Then write in the counting.

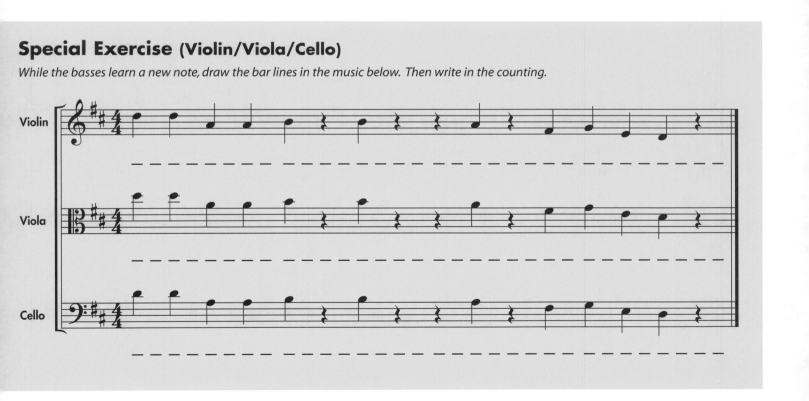

Bass

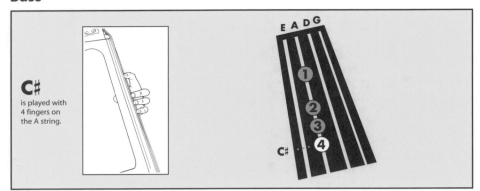

C# is played with 4 fingers on the A string.

Bass

65. LET'S READ "C#" – Review

Eighth Notes

1 &
↓ ↑

Each Eighth Note = ¹/₂ Beat
2 Eighth Notes = 1 Beat

1 & 2 &
↓ ↑ ↓ ↑

Tap your toe down on the number and up on the "&".

Two or more Eighth Notes have a *beam* across the stems.

THEORY

Teacher *Rhythm Raps* introduce new rhythms and meters. Notice the exercises that immediately follow the *Rhythm Raps* are in the same rhythm. This helps students combine their bowing, fingering, and rhythm reading skills. A suggested four-step teaching sequence for *Rhythm Raps,* as students tap their toes on the pulse, is as follows:

Step 1 – Shadow bow on rosin.
Step 2 – Bow rhythm in the air vertically, or through a tube attached to the string.
Step 3 – Bow rhythm on any open string.
Step 4 – Bow rhythm on a scale.
The piano accompaniment may be used with steps 1 and 2.

66. RHYTHM RAP *Shadow bow and count before playing.*

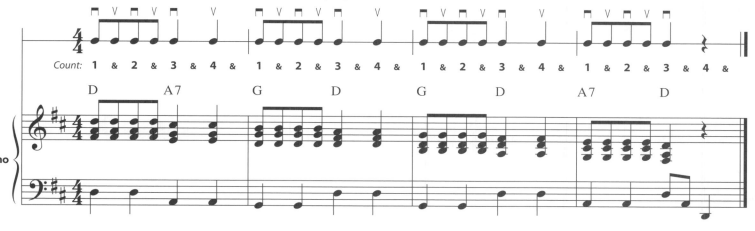

67. PEPPERONI PIZZA

68. RHYTHM RAP   *Shadow bow and count before playing.*

Piano part can be used to accompany shadow bowing and rhythm exercises.

69. D MAJOR SCALE UP

Tempo Markings   *Tempo* is the speed of music. Tempo markings are usually written above the staff, in Italian.
Allegro – Fast tempo   **Moderato** – Medium tempo   **Andante** – Slower, walking tempo

Teacher   The definition of tempo is presented on student book page 20. Only three different tempos are presented in Book 1, so that students may master their understanding.

70. HOT CROSS BUNS

Student books have repeats, not 1st and 2nd endings (until ex. 76).

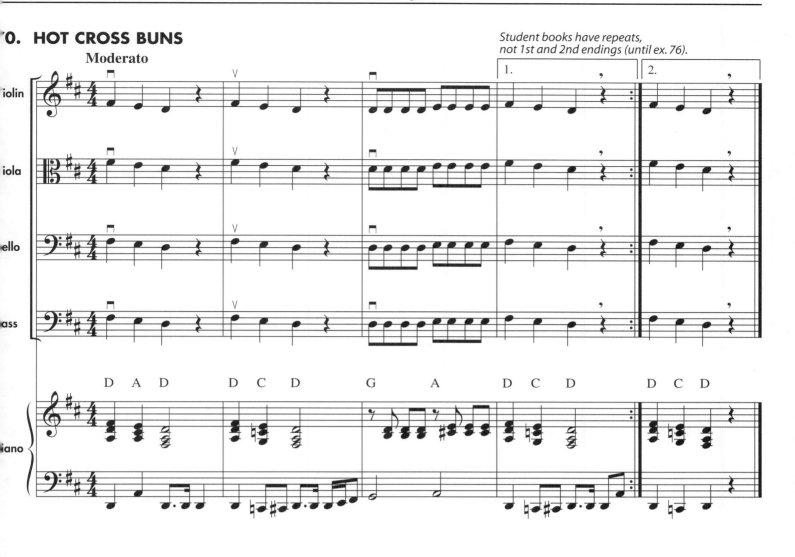

71. AU CLAIRE DE LA LUNE

French Folk Song

72. RHYTHM RAP *Shadow bow and count before playing.*

73. BUCKEYE SALUTE

Teacher Another way to help students feel a pulse is for them to conduct a meter pattern. Illustrations of meter conducting patterns are provided and can be practiced by students to develop their kinesthetic sense of pulse and consistent tempo. Please note that conducting patterns are for student use only. Teachers should be moving throughout class correcting students' playing position and posture, playing (modeling) for the students, and giving instruction. The $\frac{2}{4}$ time signature is introduced on student book page 21 and a sample 2-beat conducting pattern is shown.

$\frac{2}{4}$ **Time Signature**   **Conducting**

= **2 beats** per measure
= **Quarter** note gets one beat

Practice conducting this
two-beat pattern.

THEORY

4. RHYTHM RAP *Shadow bow and count before playing.*

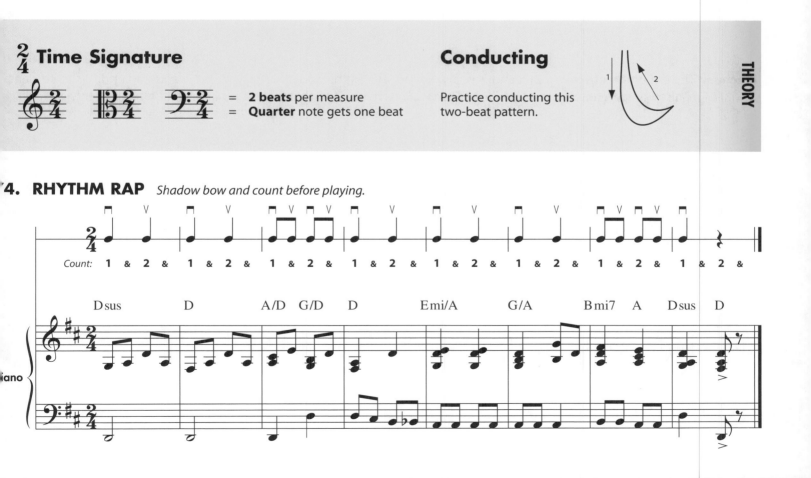

75. TWO BY TWO

THEORY

1st & 2nd Endings

Play the 1st ending the 1st time through. Then, repeat the same section of music, skip the 1st ending, and play the 2nd ending.

Teacher The definition of 1st and 2nd endings is given on student book page 21. Present 1st and 2nd endings to students as they prepare to play exercise 76, an Essential Elements Quiz that includes this new musical element.

QUIZ OBJECTIVES – FOR PETE'S SAKE
- Playing correct bow markings
- Bowing parallel to the bridge
- String Levels
- Half steps and whole steps
- 1st and 2nd endings

Review Exercises:
68. *Rhythm Rap*
74. *Rhythm Rap*
75. *Two by Two*

76. ESSENTIAL ELEMENTS QUIZ – FOR PETE'S SAKE

Essential Elements 2000 for Strings Correlated Literature

Students will enjoy playing their own special part in string orchestra arrangements. The Explorer level of *Essential Elements 2000 for Strings* series is a collection of string orchestra arrangements that only use the rhythms, bowings, and notes that are introduced on pages student book page 1–21 (Teacher Manual pages 34–119). See your Hal Leonard dealer for the latest releases.

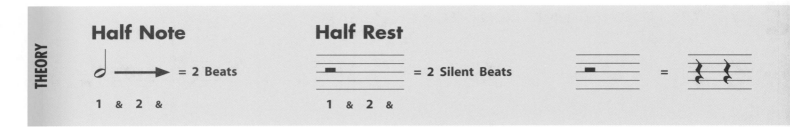

THEORY

Half Note

♩ ⟶ = 2 Beats

1 & 2 &

Half Rest

━ = 2 Silent Beats

1 & 2 &

━ = 𝄼 𝄼

Teacher   Use the suggested practice sequence for exercises 77–78 to introduce counting half notes. Be sure the students are subdividing while they are counting. The authors recommend that students count, tap, and clap each exercise before playing. You may have students shadow bow each exercise before playing as well.

Teacher   When students begin to alternate bowing quarter notes and half notes, show students how the bow should travel slower during longer notes. Students can practice this skill by bowing in the air before playing on the string. You may also use a miles-per-hour analogy to help students understand different bow speeds, e.g. slower bows travel at lower miles-per-hour than faster bows.

77. RHYTHM RAP   *Shadow bow and count before playing.*

Student books have repeats, not 1st and 2nd endings.

78. AT PIERROT'S DOOR   *Student books have repeats, not 1st and 2nd endings.*   French Folk Song

9. THE HALF COUNTS

80. GRANDPARENT'S DAY

American Folk Song

Repeat Signs

Repeat the section of music enclosed by the **repeat signs**. *(If 1st and 2nd endings are used, they are played as usual— but go back only to the first repeat sign, not to the beginning.)*

Teacher Have students point with their bows to the repeat signs and first and second endings in exercise 81. Show them other examples of music with repeats and 1st and 2nd endings. Ask students to explain how to play exercise 81 to check their understanding of repeat signs and 1st and 2nd endings.

31. MICHAEL ROW THE BOAT ASHORE

American Folk Song

Violin/Viola It is important for students to develop their left hand fourth finger facility. The following exercises and melodies are designed to help students begin to develop their fourth finger playing skill. This is critical for successful playing in the future and should be reviewed frequently. Be sure students' left hands are balanced on the third finger to make playing with the fourth finger easier.

Use rote exercises such as tapping and sliding the fourth finger while other fingers are on the string to help prepare students to use the fourth finger in their playing.

Teacher Please note that exercise 82 involves pizzicato with the left hand, not right hand.

82. TEXAS TWO-STRING

Violin/Viola *Holding your violin/viola in shoulder position, pizz. this exercise with your left hand 4th finger. 4+ = 4th finger pizz.*
Cello/Bass *Pizz. this exercise with your left hand 4th finger. 4+ = 4th finger pizz.*

Violin

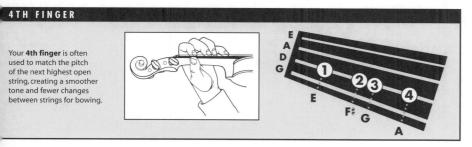

4TH FINGER

Your **4th finger** is often used to match the pitch of the next highest open string, creating a smoother tone and fewer changes between strings for bowing.

Viola

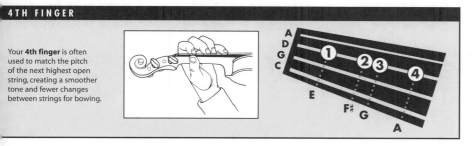

4TH FINGER

Your **4th finger** is often used to match the pitch of the next highest open string, creating a smoother tone and fewer changes between strings for bowing.

Bass

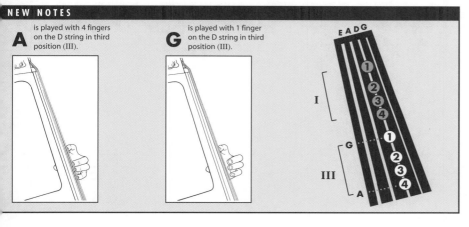

NEW NOTES

A is played with 4 fingers on the D string in third position (III).

G is played with 1 finger on the D string in third position (III).

Bass	New notes A and D in third position are introduced on student book page 23. First, have students only finger the pitches. Then, have them pizzicato the pitches. This teaching sequence will help prepare students to correctly bow the pitches.

Violin/	Fourth finger on the D string is introduced on student book page 23. The fourth finger was prepared by left-hand
Viola	pizzicato exercises on page 22. Be sure students hand shape is balanced on the third finger so that they can easily reach their fourth finger pitches.

Cello	No new notes are presented. However, consider challenging your students by having them use II ½ position to play this page. Introduce this in exercise 83 by having them place their first finger on F♯, 2nd finger on G, and 4th finger on A. They stay in this position until measure 7 when they will need to slide their hand lightly back to first position to play E. Remember to tell your students to keep the second finger behind the thumb at all times. Let them discover how they can use this new position to play other lines on this page.

83. FOUR BY FOUR

4. 4TH FINGER MARATHON

5. HIGH FLYING

HISTORY

German composer **Ludwig van Beethoven** (1770–1827) was one of the world's greatest composers. He was completely deaf by 1802. Although he could not hear music like we do, he could "hear" it in his mind. The theme of his final *Symphony No. 9* is called "Ode To Joy," and was written to the text of a poem by Friedrich von Schiller. "Ode To Joy" was featured in concerts celebrating the reunification of Germany in 1990.

Teacher Familiarize students with the music of Beethoven by playing recorded examples of his music in class, especially the last movement of his *Symphony No. 9* which includes the "Ode To Joy" theme.

QUIZ OBJECTIVES – ODE TO JOY
- Counting and playing quarter, eighth, and half notes in $\frac{4}{4}$ meter
- Changing bow speeds for different lengths of notes
- Violin/Viola fourth fingers

Review Exercises:
78. *At Pierrot's Door*
84. *Four by Four*
85. *Fourth Finger Marathon*
86. *High Flying*

86. ESSENTIAL ELEMENTS QUIZ – ODE TO JOY

Ludwig van Beethoven

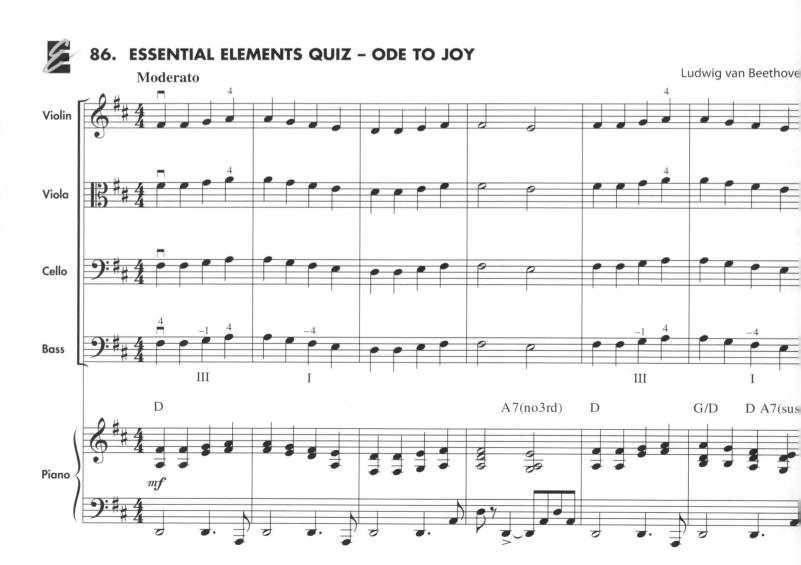

PERFORMANCE SPOTLIGHT

Teacher   A PERFORMANCE SPOTLIGHT appears on student book pages 24 and 25. The purpose of these pages is to summarize some of the principal playing skills the students have learned. These pieces may be used in a special concert performance. You may wish to show the learning process through a progression of scales, rhythm studies, duets and rounds, and/or choose to showcase the orchestra arrangements. Different styles of music are included to provide a varied musical experience for both the audience and performers.

Discuss with students proper concert etiquette for both performers and audience members. Point out that performers must practice their music until it is mastered before performing. Performers must dress appropriately for the concert, and arrive on time. Once the music is ready for performance, the audience must respect the efforts of the performer by listening quietly and attentively.

Student   Good performers are on time with their instruments and music ready, dressed appropriately, and know their music well.

87. SCALE WARM-UP

Teacher   Explain to students the organization of a round. Discuss with the class other examples of rounds common to American folk music, such as *Row, Row, Row Your Boat*.

38. FRÈRE JACQUES – Round   *(When group A reaches ②, group B begins at ①)*

French Folk Song

THEORY

Chord, Harmony

Two or more pitches sounding at the same time form a **chord** or **harmony**. Throughout this book, **A** = Melody and **B** = Harmony.

Teacher   Review the definition of chords and harmony as presented. Show and demonstrate for students different examples of chords.

Bile 'Em Cabbage Down, exercise 89, is the first orchestra arrangement in this book. All arrangements can be played with many different combinations of instruments. For the best concert performance, violins should be divided between the A and B parts, and all other instruments should play part B.

89. BILE 'EM CABBAGE DOWN – Orchestra Arrangement

0. ENGLISH ROUND

91. LIGHTLY ROW – Orchestra Arrangement

HISTORY

French composer **Jacques Offenbach** (1819–1880) was the originator of the **operetta** and played the cello. An **operetta** is a form of entertainment that combines several of the fine arts together: vocal and instrumental music, drama, dance, and visual arts. One of his most famous pieces is the "Can-Can" dance from *Orpheus And The Underworld*. This popular work was written in 1858, just three years before the start of the American Civil War (1861–1865).

Teacher Discuss the history and musical contributions of Jacques Offenbach as presented on student book page 25. Point out to students how European operettas are similar in some ways to today's American Broadway musicals. It is fun for students to find out that Offenbach, the famous composer of the *Can-Can,* was a cellist!

92. CAN-CAN – Orchestra Arrangement

Jacques Offenbach
Arr. John Higgins

What were the strong points of your performance?

Teacher   The G string and the pitches C, B, and A are introduced for the violin, viola, and cello on student book page 26. C, B, and low G are introduced for the bass since the G string already was introduced on student book page 6.

The speed of the bow should be slower on the G string than on the D and A strings. Instruct students that the lower the string, the slower the bow must travel. In addition, the bow should travel closer to the bridge on lower strings, especially on the cello and bass.

Violin

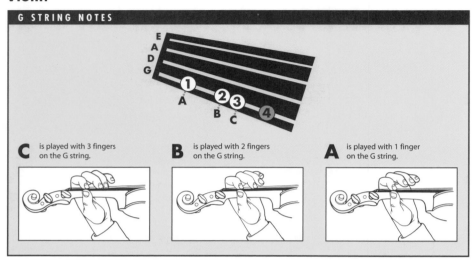

Viola

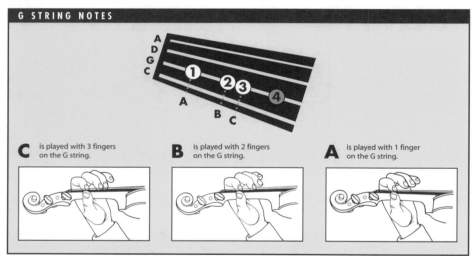

Cello

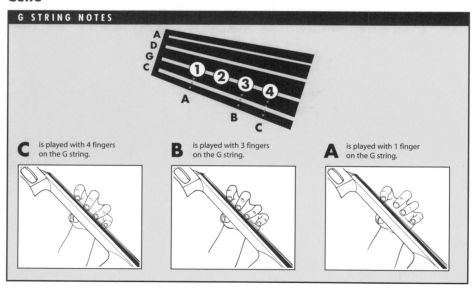

Bass

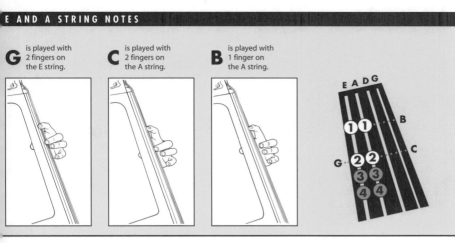

E AND A STRING NOTES

G is played with 2 fingers on the E string.

C is played with 2 fingers on the A string.

B is played with 1 finger on the A string.

Listening Skills
Play what your teacher plays. Listen carefully.

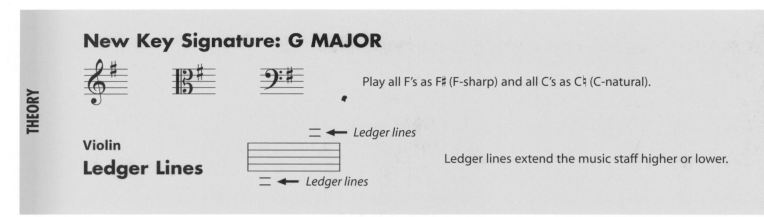

THEORY

New Key Signature: G MAJOR

Play all F's as F♯ (F-sharp) and all C's as C♮ (C-natural).

Violin
Ledger Lines

Ledger lines ← Ledger lines

Ledger lines extend the music staff higher or lower.

93. LET'S READ "G"

Play F♯'s and C♮'s in this key signature.

Violin/ When violin and viola students finger notes on the G string, their left elbow should be well under the instrument.
Viola   If their arm is properly centered underneath the instrument, students should be able to see the side of their arm
as they look through the C bout on the high string side of their instrument. Be aware that some students get
confused and attempt to swing their arm underneath the instrument to try to see their elbow. However, only the
side of the arm needs to be seen through the C bout.

Violin   Be sure all violin and viola students are forming a square with their first finger on the fingerboard when playing
Viola   "A" on the G string.

96. LET'S READ "A"

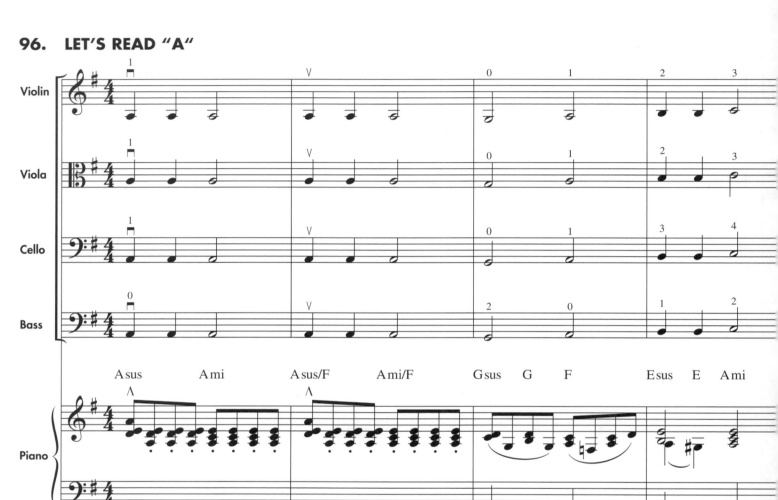

97. WALKING AROUND *Name the notes before you play.*

Teacher Check that students have written the correct name of the notes in exercise 98 before playing.

98. G MAJOR SCALE *Write the note names before you play.*

Violin/
Viola

Fourth finger D on the G string is introduced in exercise 99. Have students compare their fingered D to their open D string for tuning. Be sure their left arm is centered underneath their instrument so that they may reach the fourth finger D on the G string.

99. FOURTH FINGER D

Teacher   Have students practice the $\frac{4}{4}$ conducting pattern to reinforce their feeling and understanding of **Common Time**.

100. LOW DOWN

01. BAA BAA BLACK SHEEP

QUIZ OBJECTIVES – THIS OLD MAN
- G string notes
- Violin/Viola 4th finger D
- Counting quarter, eighth, and half notes in $\frac{4}{4}$ time

Review Exercises:
- 97. *Lift Off*
- 99. *Fourth Finger D*
- 100. *Low Down*
- 101. *Baa Baa Black Sheep*

102. ESSENTIAL ELEMENTS QUIZ – THIS OLD MAN

Moderato

American Folk Song

Teacher ¾ meter and dotted half notes are introduced on student book page 28 in the familiar key of D Major. Newly learned skills will be combined for review and reinforcement on Skill Builder pages, such as the G Major Skill Builder on page 31.

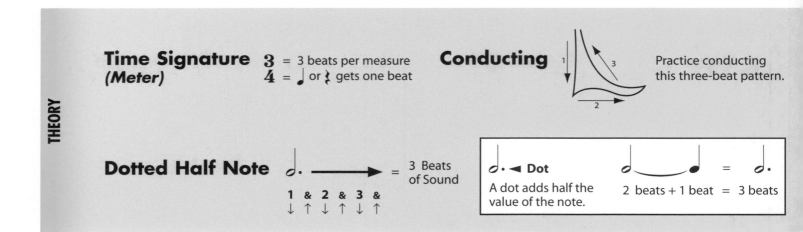

Teacher When students practice exercises on student book page 28 be sure that they count the dotted half notes carefully and move their bow slower while playing them. One suggested practice sequence is to follow the steps introduced for the previous Rhythm Raps (Teacher's Manual page 113). As students are pulling their bows, they can count 1 & 2 & etc. for the rhythm while adjusting their bow speed and tapping their foot. Alternatively, they can describe the bow speed as they are bowing, using such phrases as:

- quarter note = "fast"
- half note = "slow bow"
- dotted half note = "real slow bow"
- whole note = "real, real slow bow"

103. RHYTHM RAP *Shadow bow and count before playing.*

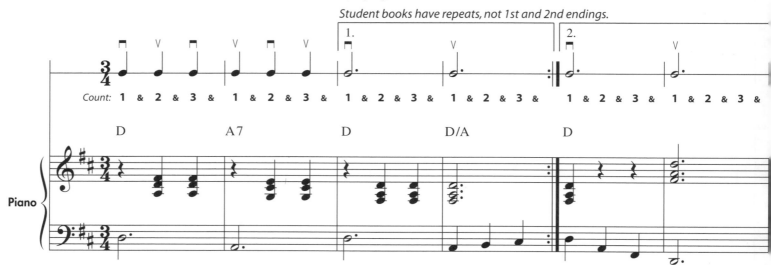

104. COUNTING THREES

Student books have repeats, not 1st and 2nd endings.

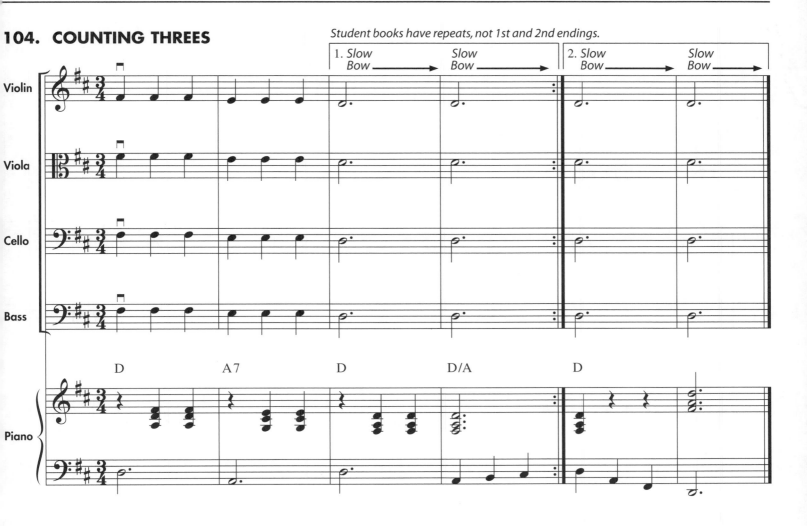

105. D MAJOR SCALE IN THREES

Bass   In *French Folk Song,* basses should play B in measure 3 with the first finger. Students may either shift their hand back to B in second and a half position, or they may pivot their hand on their thumb back to B. Remind students that the thumb slides with the hand as a unit when shifting. Instruct them that when pivoting, the thumb does not slide along the neck of the instrument, but pivots on the pad of the thumb.

Bass
New Position – II½   (Second and a half position – first finger on B.)

106. FRENCH FOLK SONG

French Folk Song

QUIZ OBJECTIVES – SAILOR'S SONG

- $\frac{3}{4}$ time signature
- Counting dotted half notes
- Changing bow speeds for different note lengths

Review Exercises:

104. *Counting Threes*
105. *D Scale in Threes*
106. *French Folk Song*

107. ESSENTIAL ELEMENTS QUIZ – SAILOR'S SONG

English Sea Song

△ *Write in the correct time signature before you begin.*

Tie  A **tie** is a curved line that connects notes of the **same** pitch. Play a single note for the combined counts of the tied notes.  THEORY

Teacher Ties and slurs are presented on student book page 29. Discuss with students the difference between a tie and a slur.

108. FIT TO BE TIED

THEORY | **Slur**

A **slur** is a curved line that connects two or more **different** pitches. Play slurred notes together in the same bow stroke.

Teacher To help prepare to learn slurring, have students trill while pulling their bow in one direction. Incorporate slurred examples in their listening skill echoes. Also, consider adding slurs to the D major scale and to previously learned pieces. Another effective way to introduce slurring is to have students practice bowing two detached notes in the same direction, eventually eliminating the bow stop between the pitches, e.g.

109. STOP AND GO

110. SLURRING ALONG

111. SMOOTH SAILING

12. D MAJOR SLURS

Teacher   Tell students that their string crossings should be smooth. Show them that in slurred string crossings their bow should follow the natural curvature of their instrument's bridge. Check to see if their right arm and bow hand are changing levels when changing strings.

113. CROSSING STRINGS

114. GLIDING BOWS

15. UPSIDE DOWN

THEORY

Upbeat

A note (or notes) that appears before the first full measure is called an **upbeat** (or **pickup**). The remaining beats are found in the last measure.

Teacher   Read the definition of upbeat presented on student book page 30. Upbeats are sometimes called pick-up notes.

116. SONG FOR MARIA

Latin American music combines the folk music from South and Central America, the Caribbean Islands, African, Spanish, and Portuguese cultures. Melodies often feature a lively accompaniment by drums, maracas, and claves. Latin American styles have become part of jazz, classical, and rock music.

HISTORY

D.C. al Fine

Play until you see the **D.C. al Fine**. Then go back to the beginning and play until you see **Fine** *(fee'- nay)*. **D.C.** is the abbreviation for **Da Capo**, the Italian term for "return to the beginning." **Fine** is the Italian word for "the finish."

THEORY

Teacher   Play recorded examples of Latin, Caribbean, African, Spanish, and Portuguese music to familiarize students with these musical styles.

17. BANANA BOAT SONG

Caribbean Folk Song

118. FIROLIRALERA – Orchestra Arrangement

Mexican Folk Son[g]
Arr. John Higgin[s]

SKILL BUILDERS – G Major

Teacher The purpose of EE SKILL BUILDERS is to summarize and reinforce playing skills that have been recently learned. The exercises are in sequential order of playing difficulty. Students should master each of the exercises in the EE SKILL BUILDERS before proceeding to the next one.

119.

120.

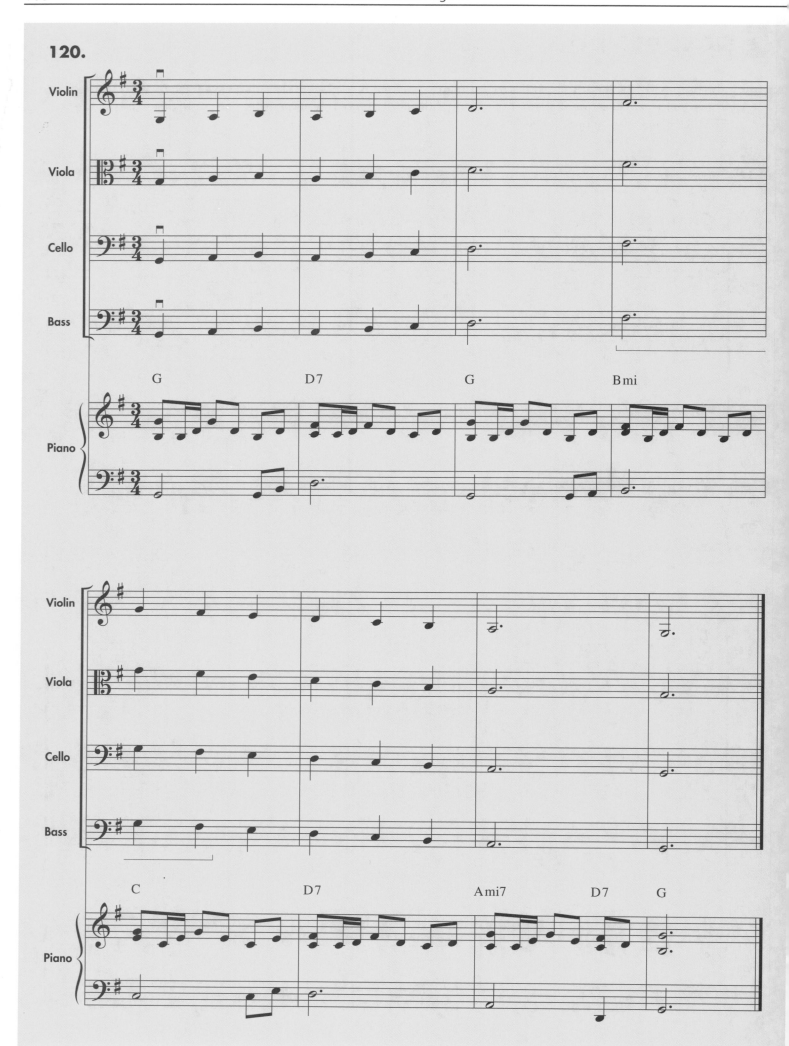

121.

122.

123.

124.

Far Eastern music comes from Malaysia, Indonesia, China and other areas. Historians believe the first orchestras, known as **gamelans**, existed in this region as early as the 1st century B.C. Today's gamelans include rebabs (spiked fiddles), gongs, xylophones, and a wide variety of percussion instruments.

125. JINGLI NONA

Far Eastern Folk Song

Teacher F♮ and C♮ are introduced on student book pages 32 and 33. To help prepare students to finger F♮, which requires a new finger pattern for the violin and viola, have students tap their second finger while keeping their other fingers on the string. Also, have them slide their second finger back and forth between their first and third fingers, while keeping all of their fingers on the string. Both of these rote exercises help develop finger flexibility and independence of fingers. In addition, prepare and reinforce student aural learning of F♮ by incorporating the following *Listening Skills* echo patterns for students.

Violin/Viola

Violin

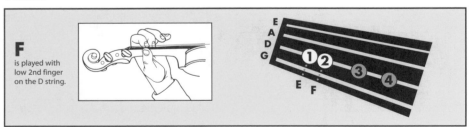

Viola

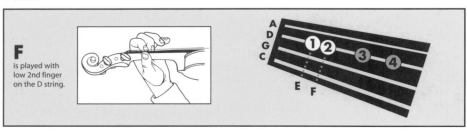

Cello

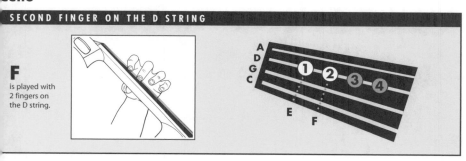

SECOND FINGER ON THE D STRING

F
is played with
2 fingers on
the D string.

Bass

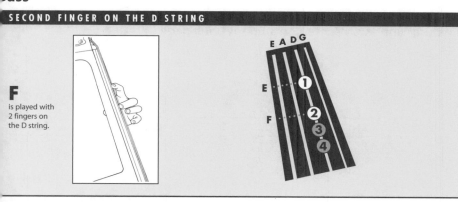

SECOND FINGER ON THE D STRING

F
is played with
2 fingers on
the D string.

Listening Skills

Play what your teacher plays. Listen carefully.

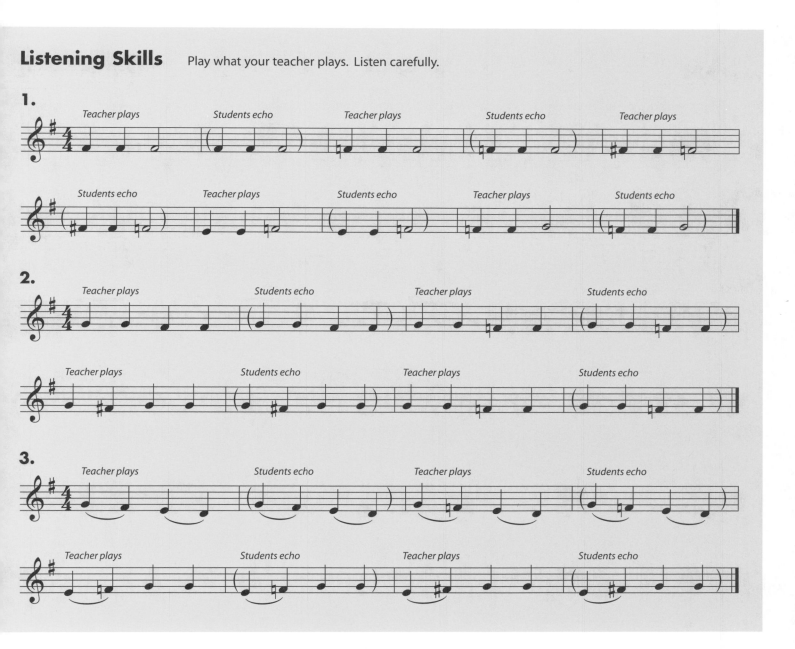

Natural ♮   A **natural** sign cancels a flat (♭) or sharp (♯) and remains in effect for the entire measure.

Teacher   Review with students the definition of a natural sign as presented on student book page 32.

126. LET'S READ "F" (F-natural)

Half Step

A **half step** is the smallest distance between two notes.

Whole Step

A **whole step** is two half steps combined.

Teacher Read and discuss the definitions of half and whole steps found on student book page 32. Present some rote listening-skill echoes to students that incorporate both half and whole steps. Also, have students mark the half steps in exercises 128, 129, and 132 to reinforce their understanding of half and whole steps.

27. HALF-STEPPIN' AND WHOLE STEPPIN'

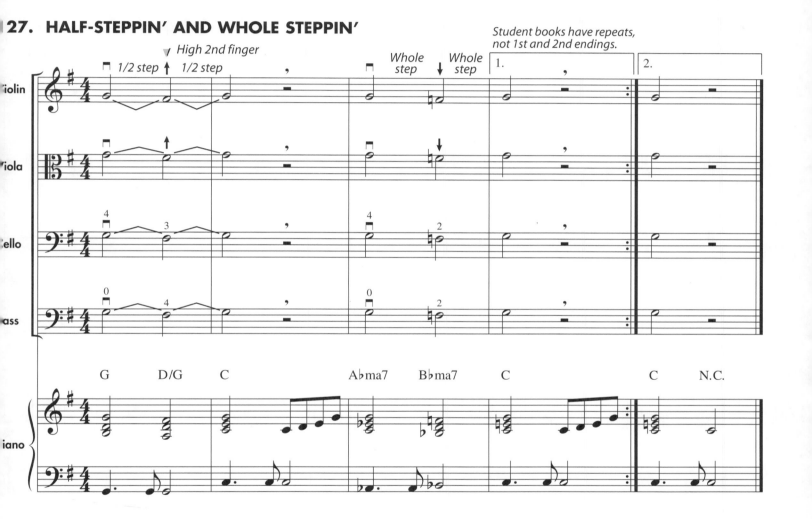

128. SPY GUY

129. MINOR DETAILS

Violin

NEW FINGER PATTERN

Low 2nd Finger On The A String

Shape your left hand on the A string as shown.

C

is played with low 2nd finger on the A string.

Viola

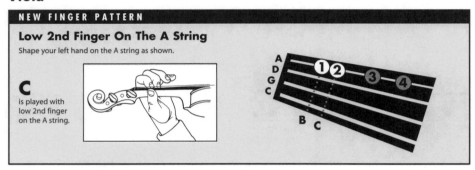

NEW FINGER PATTERN

Low 2nd Finger On The A String

Shape your left hand on the A string as shown.

C

is played with low 2nd finger on the A string.

Cello

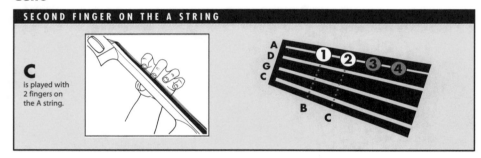

SECOND FINGER ON THE A STRING

C

is played with 2 fingers on the A string.

Bass

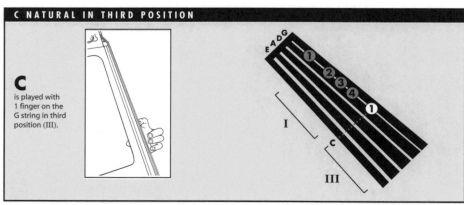

C NATURAL IN THIRD POSITION

C

is played with 1 finger on the G string in third position (III).

131. HALF STEP AND WHOLE STEP REVIEW

Student books have repeats, not 1st and 2nd endings

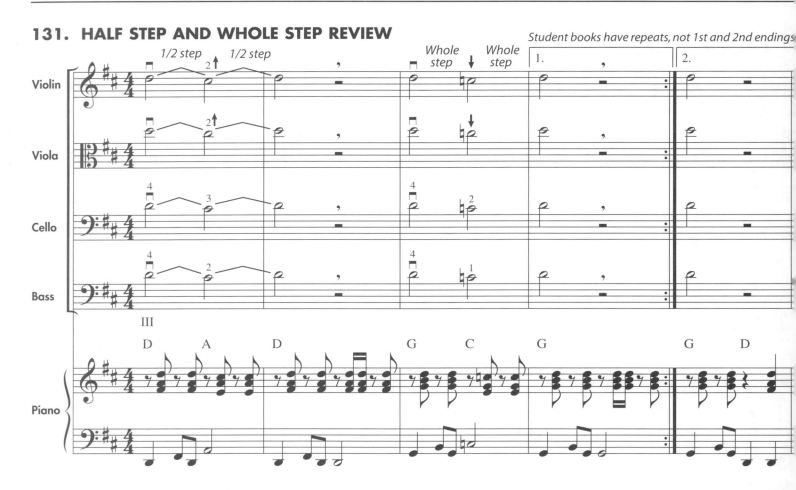

Chromatics

Chromatic notes are altered with sharps, flats, and naturals. A chromatic pattern is two or more notes in a sequence of half steps.

132. CHROMATIC MOVES

33. THE STETSON SPECIAL

134. BLUEBIRD'S SONG

Texas Folk Song

Essential Elements 2000 for Strings **Correlated Literature**

The Performer level of *Essential Elements 2000 for Strings* is a collection of string orchestra arrangements that only uses the rhythms, bowings, and notes introduced on student pages 1–33 (Teacher Manual pages 39–182). Contact your local music dealer for more information.

New Key Signature: C MAJOR

All notes are naturals.

THEORY

Bass
New Position – II　(Second finger on B, fourth finger on C.)

Teacher Student book page 34 introduces the key of C major. A one-octave C major scale is presented, along with three melodies in C Major. This involves introducing second-finger B and fourth-finger C in second position on the double bass.

135. C MAJOR SCALE – Round

Duet   A composition with two different parts, played together.

136. SPLIT DECISION – Duet

137. OAK HOLLOW

38. A-TISKET, A-TASKET

HISTORY

In the second half of the 1800s many composers tried to express the spirit of their own country by writing music with a distinct national flavor. Listen to the music of Russian composers such as Borodin, Tchaikovsky, and Rimsky-Korsakov. They often used folk songs and dance rhythms to convey their nationalism. Describe the sounds you hear.

Teacher   Discuss the concept of nationalistic music. Play recordings of music by Russian composers, Borodin, Tchaikovsky and Rimsky-Korsakov. Discuss how their music is often nationalistic. Introduce recordings of other nationalistic compositions such as *Finlandia* by Sibelius and *The Moldau* by Smetana.

QUIZ OBJECTIVES – RUSSIAN FOLK TUNE
- F natural
- C natural
- Violin/Viola 4th finger
- Andante tempo

Review Exercises:
129. *Minor Details*
133. *The Stetson Special*
135. *C Major Scale*
138. *Oak Hollow*

139. ESSENTIAL ELEMENTS QUIZ – RUSSIAN FOLK TUNE

Alert: This page mixes finger patterns. Watch for low second finger (C♮) and high second finger (F♯).

Teacher   Student book page 35 reinforces students' knowledge of the notes F♮ and C♮ by contrasting them with F♯ and C♯ within melodies. Have students play C♮ and C♯ and F♮ and F♯ as a review in listening-skill rote echoes before beginning to practice the melodies on this page.

140. BINGO

18th Century English Game Song

English composer **Thomas Tallis** (1505–1585) served as royal court composer during the reigns of Henry VIII, Edward VI, Mary, and Elizabeth I. Composers and artists during this era wanted to recreate the artistic and scientific glories of ancient Greece and Rome. The great artist Michelangelo painted the Sistine Chapel during Tallis' lifetime. **Rounds** and **canons** were popular forms of music during the early 16th century. Divide into groups, and play or sing the *Tallis Canon* as a 4-part round.

Teacher   Have students use note names or solfeggio to sing the *Tallis Canon*.

41. TALLIS CANON – Round

THEORY

Theme and Variations

Theme and Variations is a musical form where a theme, or melody, is followed by different versions of the same theme.

Teacher Contrast the differences between the musical forms of Rounds and Theme and Variations as students prepare to play exercise 142.

In exercise 142 students are given the opportunity to compose their own variation on the melody *Skip to My Lou.* Specify musical parameters to help them compose their variation. For example, suggest sample rhythms or slurring that they can use.

142. VARIATIONS ON A FAMILIAR SONG

Student **Variation 2** – *make up your own variation.*

Teacher   Teach students Exercise 143 *The Birthday Song* as printed. Students will notice that the typical two-eighth note pick up is missing from the traditional *Happy Birthday* melody. Have them add this rhythm when performing as a part of their creativity development.

143. ESSENTIAL CREATIVITY – THE BIRTHDAY SONG

Student   *Now play the line again and create your own rhyth*

Teacher Student book page 36 introduces C string pitches to viola and cello students. Once learned, the cellos and violas will be prepared to play two-octave C major scales on their instruments. Be sure to incorporate listening-skill rote echoes in your teaching to help develop students' aural understanding of C string pitches.

It is important for the violas and cellos to have enough time in class to develop skill playing on their C string. Even though the following exercises are a review of previously learned pitches for the violin and bass, students must understand the importance of being patient while their classmates learn new notes. To help, a message about the importance of team work in the orchestra and special note and story writing exercises are provided in violin and bass student books.

Introduce C string pitches through listening exercises. Violin and bass students echo the pitches on their instruments in different octaves.

Viola

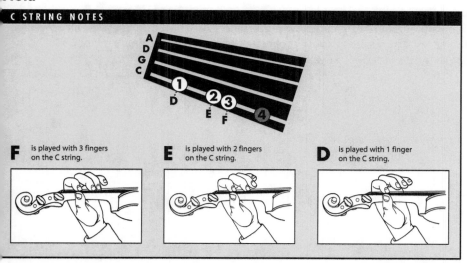

Cello

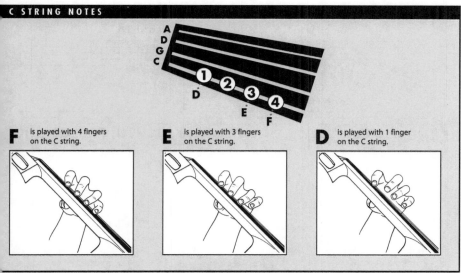

Violin

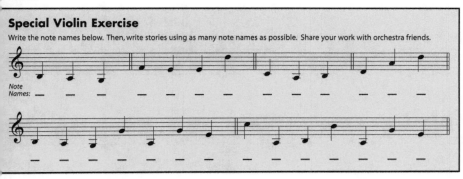

Bass

Violin/Bass

Team Work

Great musicians give encouragement to their fellow performers. Viola and cello players will now learn new challenging notes. The success of your orchestra depends on everyone's talent and patience. Play your best as these sections advance their musical technique.

Listening Skills

Play what your teacher plays. Listen carefully.

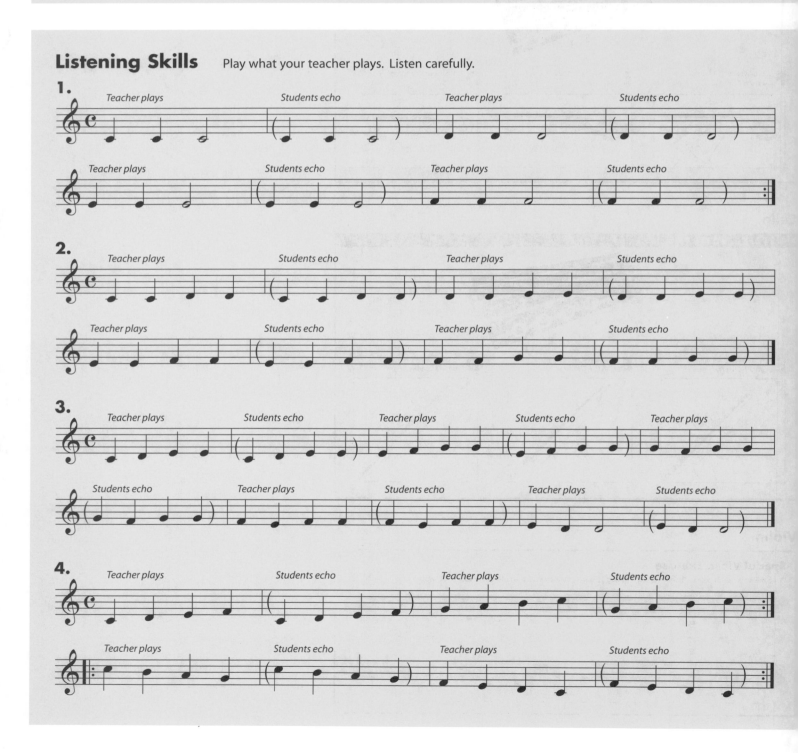

144. LET'S READ "C"

145. LET'S READ "F"

146. LET'S READ "E"

147. LET'S READ "D"

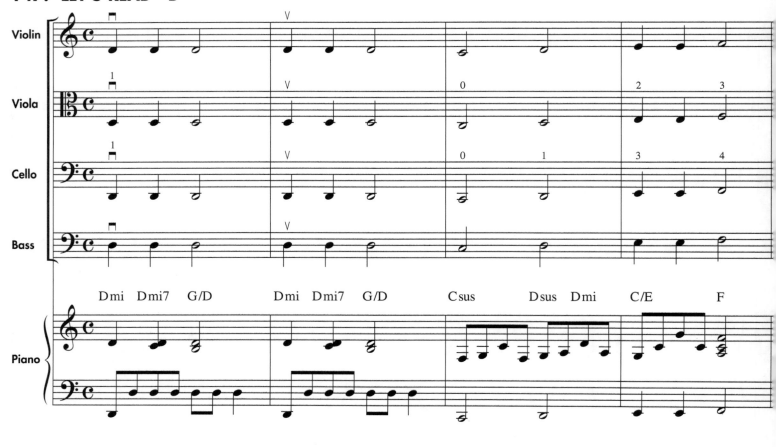

148. SIDE BY SIDE *Name the notes before you play.*

149. C MAJOR SCALE

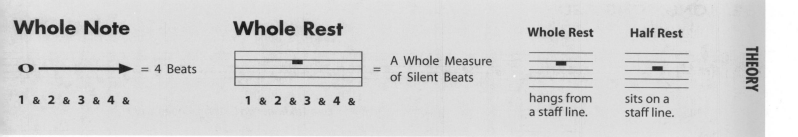

Whole Note

o ——▶ = 4 Beats

1 & 2 & 3 & 4 &

Whole Rest

= A Whole Measure of Silent Beats

1 & 2 & 3 & 4 &

Whole Rest

hangs from a staff line.

Half Rest

sits on a staff line.

THEORY

Teacher Practice with students the *Rhythm Rap*, exercise 150, using the suggested practice techniques from previous *Rhythm Raps*. Remind students that they must pull their bows very slowly and count carefully when playing whole notes. Emphasize the difference in placement on the staff of a whole rest and a half rest.

150. RHYTHM RAP *Shadow bow and count before playing.*

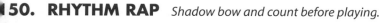

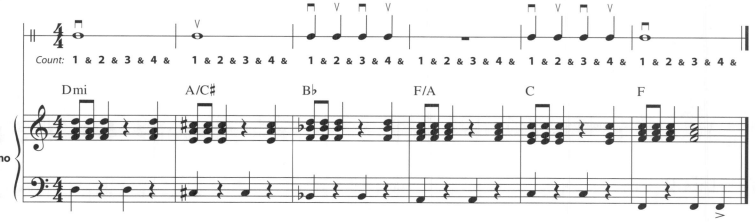

151. SLOW BOWS

152. LONG, LONG AGO

T. H. Baily

4 ◄ *4th finger on C string = open G pitch*

Arpeggio

An **arpeggio** is a chord whose pitches are played one at a time. Your first arpeggio uses the 1st, 3rd, 5th, and 8th steps from the C major scale.

Teacher Discuss the definition of arpeggio. Practice the arpeggio in the last four measures before playing the entire exercise.

53. C MAJOR SCALE AND ARPEGGIO

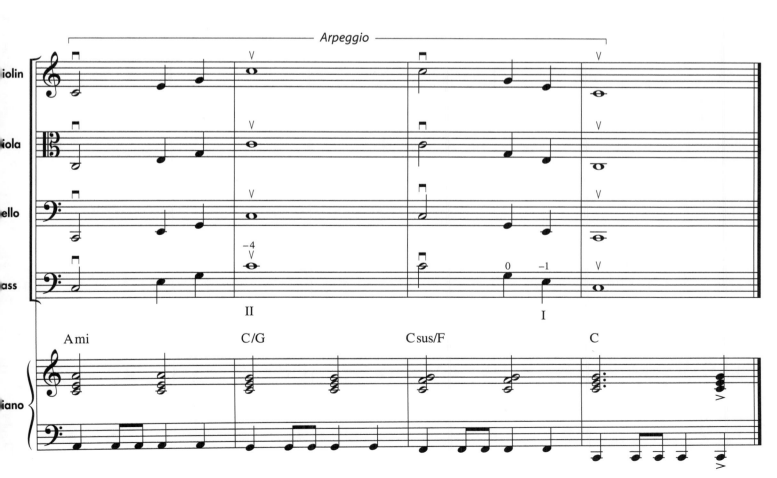

154. LISTEN TO OUR SECTIONS

155. MONDAY'S MELODY

Traditional Folk Song

Teacher   The E string and the pitches A, G, and F♯ are introduced for violin on student book page 38. Fourth finger E on the A string is introduced on the viola. No new notes for the cello are introduced, while the E string and F♯ are introduced for the bass. Special writing exercises are provided for the viola and cello.

Violin

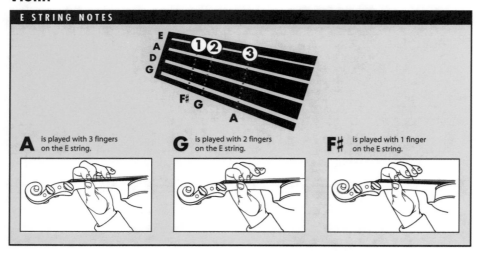

Viola

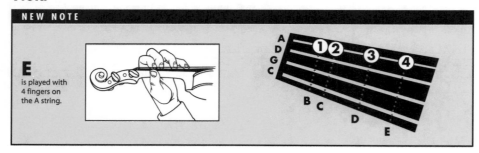

Cello

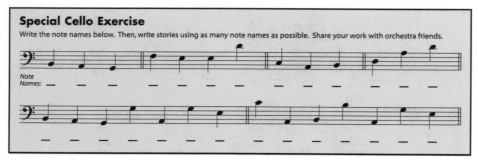

Bass

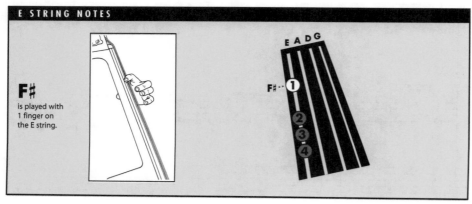

Viola, Cello
Team Work

Great musicians give encouragement to their fellow performers. Violin and bass players will now learn new challenging notes. The success of your orchestra depends on everyone's talent and patience. Play your best as these sections advance their musical technique.

Teacher Play the following *Listening Skills* patterns to begin introducing the new notes to students. Remember that the patterns may be played on any instrument.

Listening Skills Play what your teacher plays. Listen carefully.

156. LET'S READ "E"

Viola

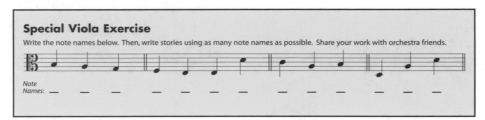

Special Viola Exercise
Write the note names below. Then, write stories using as many note names as possible. Share your work with orchestra friends.

Viola
Team Work

Great musicians give encouragement to their fellow performers. Violin and bass players will now learn new challenging notes. The success of your orchestra depends on everyone's talent and patience. Play your best as these sections advance their musical technique.

157. LET'S READ "A"

158. LET'S READ "G"

159. LET'S READ "F♯" (F-sharp)

160. MOVING ALONG *Name the notes before you play.*

161. G MAJOR SCALE

162. SHEPHERD'S HEY

English Folk Song

163. BIG ROCK CANDY MOUNTAIN

American Folk Song

Violin

Teacher   The note B is introduced for the violin on student book page 39. Use the following *Listening Skills* echo patterns to help students learn this new pitch.

Listening Skills   Play what your teacher plays. Listen carefully.

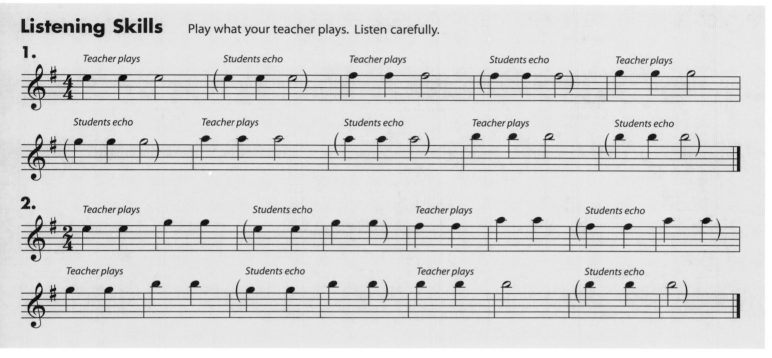

Violin

B

164. LET'S READ "B"

165. ICE SKATING

eacher Familiarize students with different examples of music by Johannes Brahms. Play an excerpt of the melody in exercise 166 from a recording of the *Academic Festival Overture*.

QUIZ OBJECTIVES – ACADEMIC FESTIVAL OVERTURE THEME
- E string notes
- Upbeat

Review Exercises:
  162. *Shepherd's Hey*
  163. *Big Rock Candy Mountain*
  165. *Ice Skating*

166. ESSENTIAL ELEMENTS QUIZ – ACADEMIC FESTIVAL OVERTURE THEME

Johannes Brahms

Staccato notes are marked with a dot above or below the note. A staccato note is played with a stopped bow stroke. Listen for a space between staccato notes.

Teacher Staccato bowing is introduced at the top of student book page 40. Demonstrate the stroke for students. Point out how the staccato stroke begins with a slight pinch of the index finger on the bow stick. You may have students just practice the pinching motion at the balance point of their bow as a separate task before they pull the bow to start the staccato stroke. Have students practice their staccato bowing on open strings first, then on familiar scales.

167. PLAY STACCATO

168. ARKANSAS TRAVELER

Southern American Folk Song

Teacher   *EE SKILL BUILDERS – G MAJOR* appears on student book page 40. Its purpose is to reinforce students' understanding of G major, especially the upper octave incorporating the E string on the violin.

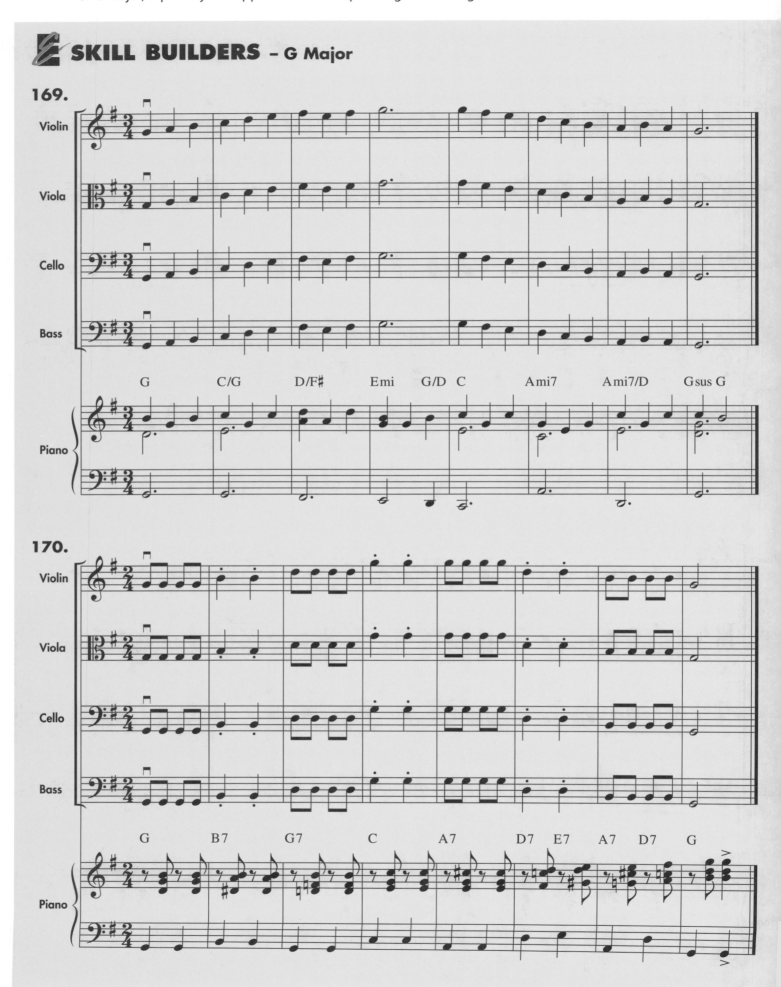

SKILL BUILDERS – G Major

171.

SKILL BUILDERS – G Major

172.

Hooked Bowing

Hooked bowing is two or more notes played in the same direction with a stop between each note.

Teacher Demonstrate hooked bowing for students. Explain that hooked staccato notes simply involve bowing two staccato pitches in the same direction. As students practice their hooked bowing, their bows should completely stop between pitches. Practice hooked bowing on open strings first and then on familiar scales, as in exercises 174 and 175.

74. HOOKED ON D MAJOR

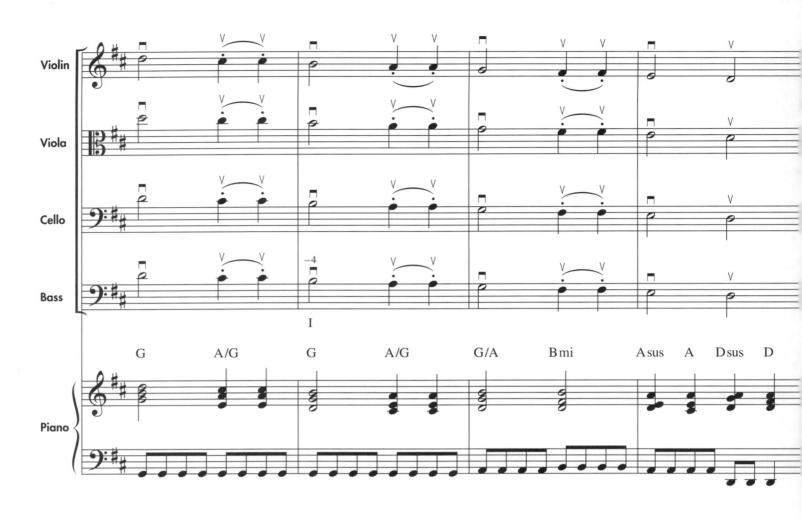

175. WALTZING BOWS

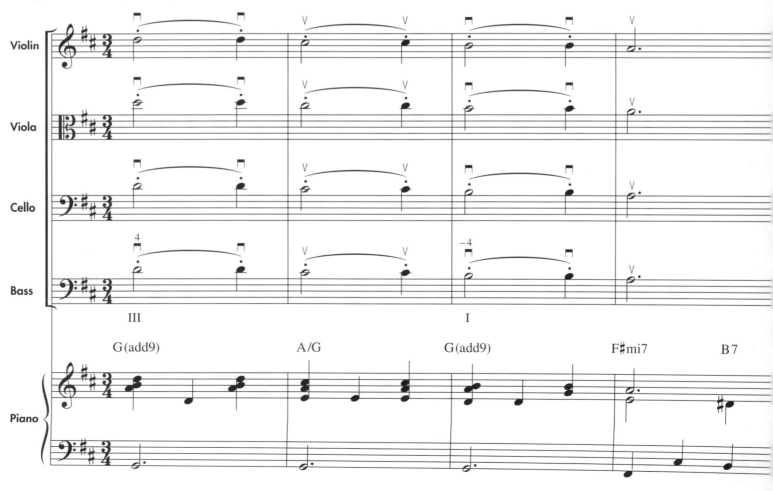

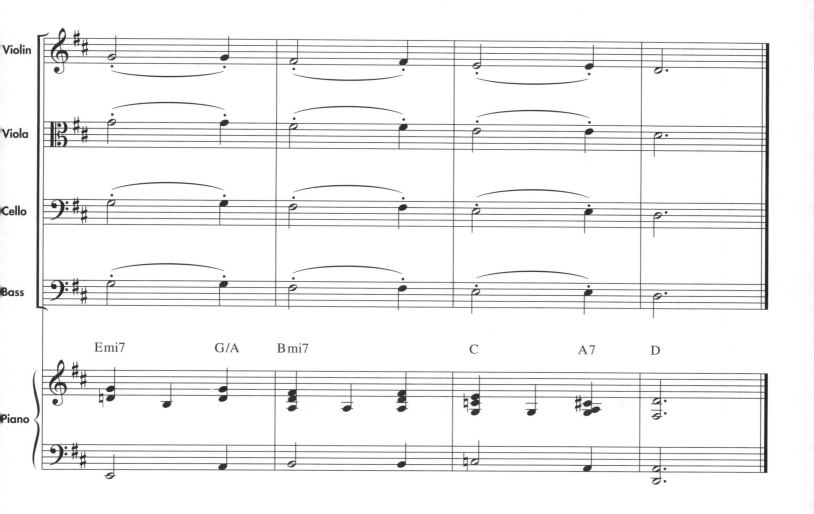

176. POP GOES THE WEASEL

American Folk Song

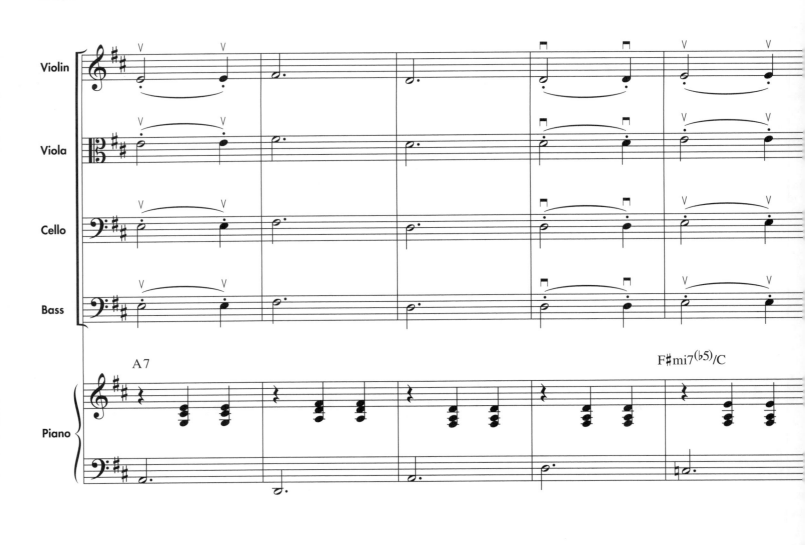

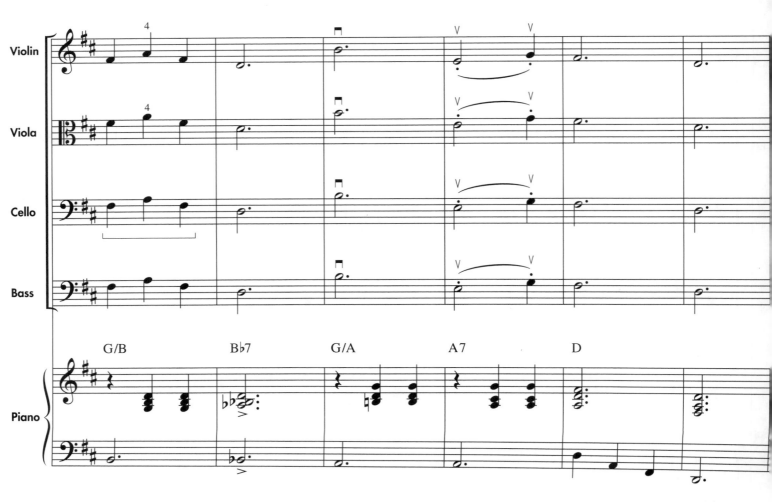

Teacher *EE SKILL BUILDERS – C MAJOR* will reinforce students' understanding of C major, especially the lower octave incorporating the C string on the viola and cello.

SKILL BUILDERS – C Major

Dynamics

Dynamics tell us what volume to play or sing.

f (forte)   Play loudly. Add more weight to the bow.

p (piano)   Play softly. Remove weight from the bow.

Teacher   The definition of forte and piano dynamics is given at the top of student book page 42. Play listening skill exercises incorporating different dynamic levels in preparation for exercises 181 and 182.

181. FORTE AND PIANO

Student books have repeats, not 1st and 2nd endings.

Teacher Familiarize students with the music of Franz Josef Haydn by playing recorded examples of his music, including the second movement of his Symphony No. 94 that contains *The Surprise Symphony* theme in exercise 182.

182. SURPRISE SYMPHONY THEME

Franz Josef Haydn

Teacher   *EE SKILL BUILDERS – SCALES and ARPEGGIOS* reviews and reinforces all the scales, and their related arpeggios, presented in this book.

SKILL BUILDERS – Scales and Arpeggios

Add your own dynamics to any of the lines below.

183. D MAJOR

Student books have repeats, not 1st and 2nd endings.

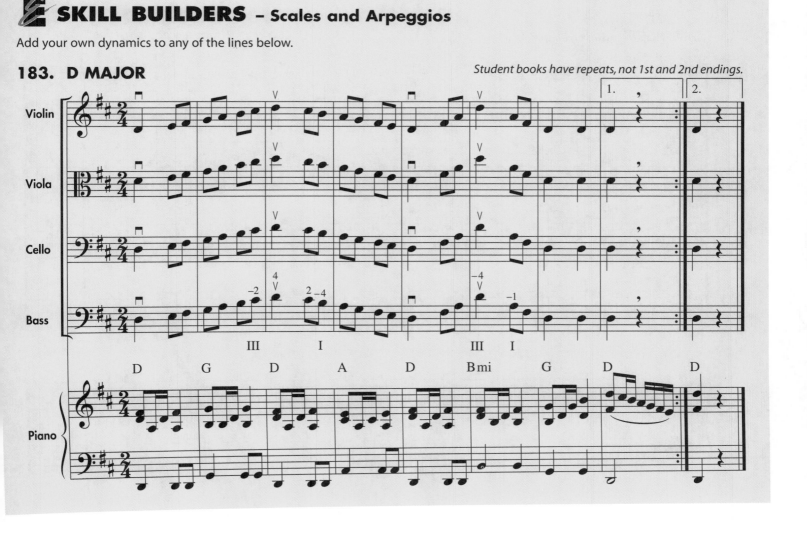

SKILL BUILDERS – Scales and Arpeggios

184. G MAJOR   *Student books have repeats, not 1st and 2nd endings.*

185. G MAJOR *(Upper Octave – violin)*   *Student books have repeats, not 1st and 2nd endings.*

SKILL BUILDERS – Scales and Arpeggios

186. C MAJOR *Student books have repeats, not 1st and 2nd endings.*

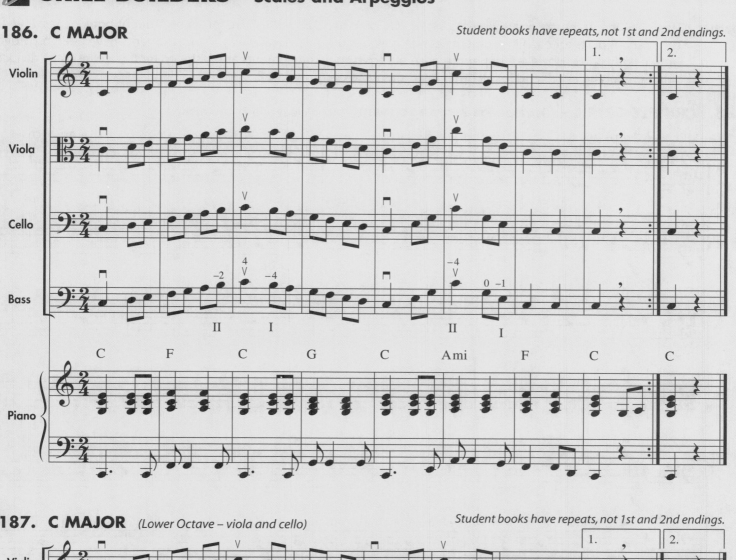

187. C MAJOR *(Lower Octave – viola and cello)* *Student books have repeats, not 1st and 2nd endings.*

PERFORMANCE SPOTLIGHT

Teacher The following orchestra arrangements in the *PERFORMANCE SPOTLIGHT* are found on student book pages 43–44. The A and B parts for each instrument section may be combined in any way. All instruments have been provided with melody parts. However, for performance purposes the arrangements are designed for the violins to be divided between parts A and B and for all other instruments to perform part B.

188. CRIPPLE CREEK – Orchestra Arrangement (A = Melody and B = Harmony)

American Folk Song
Arr. Michael Allen

THEORY

Africa is a large continent made up of many nations, and African folk music is as diverse as its many cultures. This folk song is from Kenya. The words describe warriors as they prepare for battle. Listen to examples of African folk music and describe the sound.

Teacher   Play recordings of African folk music and have students describe the sounds they hear.

189. TEKELE LOMERIA – Orchestra Arrangement

Kenyan Warrior Song
Arr. John Higgins

PERFORMANCE SPOTLIGHT

HISTORY

Italian composer **Gioachino Rossini** (1792–1868) wrote some of the world's favorite operas. "William Tell" was Rossini's last opera, and its popular theme is still heard on television.

Teacher Familiarize students with the music of Gioachino Rossini by playing recorded examples of his works in class. He wrote many lively overtures, such as the *Overture to William Tell,* which are interesting for young students to hear.

190. WILLIAM TELL OVERTURE – Orchestra Arrangement

Gioachino Rossini
Arr. John Higgins

191. ROCKIN' STRINGS – Orchestra Arrangement

John Higgin

PERFORMANCE SPOTLIGHT

192. SIMPLE GIFTS – Orchestra Arrangement

Shaker Folk Song
Arr. John Higgins

Essential Elements 2000 for Strings Correlated Literature

Students will enjoy playing their own special part in other string orchestra arrangements. The Artist level of *Essential Elements 2000 for Strings* series is a collection of string orchestra arrangements that only use the rhythms, bowings, and notes that are introduced on pages student book page 1–42 (Teacher Manual pages 39–233). See your Hal Leonard dealer for the latest releases.

PERFORMANCE SPOTLIGHT – Violin

Solo with Piano Accompaniment

A solo is a composition written for one player, often with piano accompaniment. This solo was written by **Johann Sebastian Bach** (1685–1750). You and a piano accompanist can perform for the orchestra, your school, your family, and at other occasions. When you have learned the piece well, try memorizing it. Performing for an audience is an exciting part of being involved in music.

Teacher Each instrument has its own solo as a part of *PERFORMANCE SPOTLIGHT* on student book page 46. The solos may be used as a new musical experience for the string student and as a reward for effort and achievement. The corresponding piano accompaniments are included in each student book. Consider featuring these solos on concerts, performed by individual students or by instrument sections.

193. MINUET NO. 1 – Solo

Johann Sebastian Bach
Arr. John Higgins

PERFORMANCE SPOTLIGHT – Viola

Solo with Piano Accompaniment

A solo is a composition written for one player, often with piano accompaniment. This solo was written by **Johann Sebastian Bach** (1685–1750). You and a piano accompanist can perform for the orchestra, your school, your family, and at other occasions. When you have learned the piece well, try memorizing it. Performing for an audience is an exciting part of being involved in music.

193. MINUET IN C – Solo

Johann Sebastian Bach
Arr. John Higgins

PERFORMANCE SPOTLIGHT – Cello

Solo with Piano Accompaniment

A solo is a composition written for one player, often with piano accompaniment. This solo was written by **Johann Sebastian Bach** (1685–1750). You and a piano accompanist can perform for the orchestra, your school, your family, and at other occasions. When you have learned the piece well, try memorizing it. Performing for an audience is an exciting part of being involved in music.

193. MINUET NO. 2 – Solo

Johann Sebastian Bach
Arr. John Higgins

PERFORMANCE SPOTLIGHT - Bass

Solo with Piano Accompaniment

A solo is a composition written for one player, often with piano accompaniment. This solo was written by **Johann Sebastian Bach** (1685–1750). You and a piano accompanist can perform for the orchestra, your school, your family, and at other occasions. When you have learned the piece well, try memorizing it. Performing for an audience is an exciting part of being involved in music.

193. MARCH IN D – Solo

Johann Sebastian Bach
Arr. John Higgins

THEORY

Improvisation

Improvisation is the art of freely creating your own music as you play.

Teacher   Students are given the opportunity to apply rhythms of their choice to the pitches provided In exercise 194, *Rhythm Jam.* Remind students that there must be a total of four beats in each measure. Inform them that they can use a variety of bowings including slurs, staccato and/or hooked bowings. Give students the opportunity to perform their examples in class. Some may even be selected to perform on a concert to reinforce and reward student creativity.

194. RHYTHM JAM   *Using the following notes, improvise your own rhythms.*

Teacher Give students parameters when they begin to create their improvised melody in exercise 195. For example, instruct students to select pitches only from the D major scale. Also, remind them that there must be four beats in each measure. Consider limiting rhythmic values that students may use to help them in their creativity, e.g. using only quarter and half notes, or quarter and eighth notes. Suggest that their melody will sound more natural if it begins and ends on the pitch D. Have students write out their improvised melodies to reinforce their note and rhythmic reading. Allow students to perform their melodies while accompanied by other students playing the B line. Select students to play their newly created, improvised melodies on a concert.

195. INSTANT MELODY *Using the following notes, improvise your own melody (Line A), to go with the accompaniment (Line B).*

Teacher   The following fingering charts appear on page 47 of each student book.

Violin

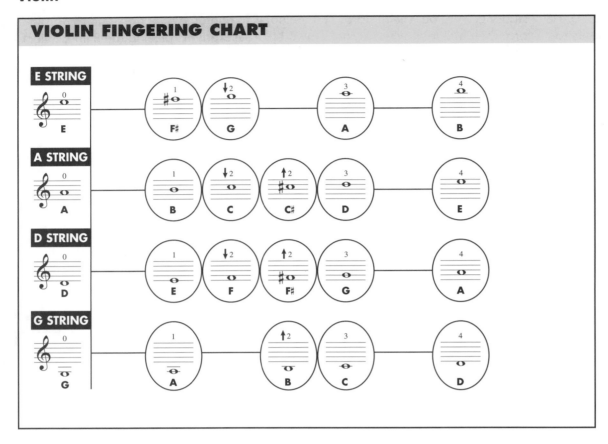

Viola

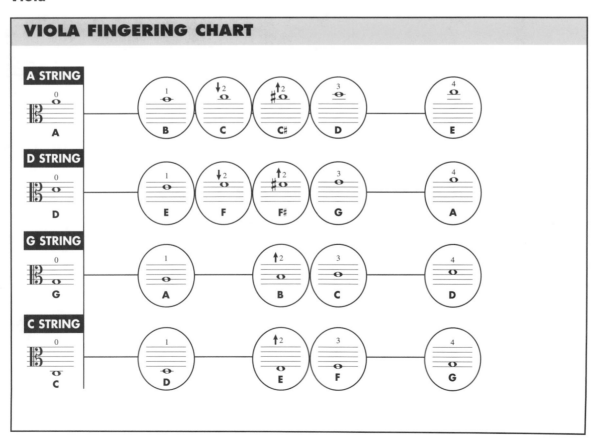

Cello

CELLO FINGERING CHART

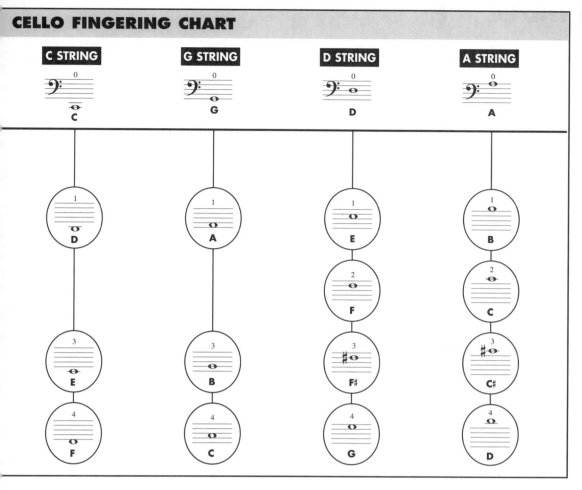

Bass

DOUBLE BASS FINGERING CHART

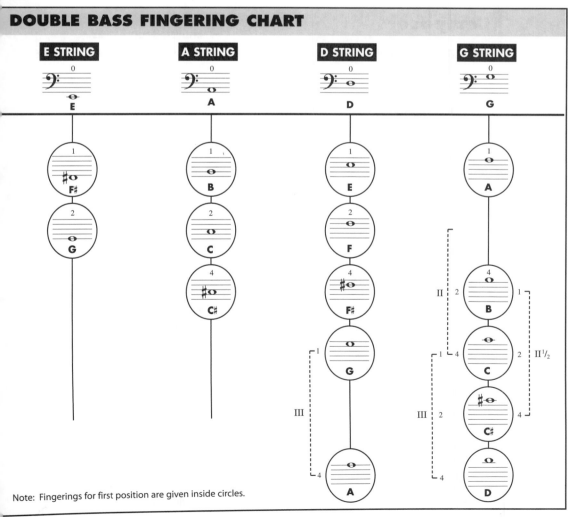

Note: Fingerings for first position are given inside circles.

REFERENCE INDEX

Definitions (pg.)

Allegro   20

Alto Clef   5 (viola)

Andante   20

Arco   16

Arpeggio   37

Bar Lines   4

Bass Clef   5 (cello & bass)

Beat   4

Bow Lift   17

Chord   24

Chromatics   33

Common Time   27

Counting   5

D.C. al Fine   30

Dotted Half Note   28

Double Bar   5

Down Bow   13

Duet   34

Dynamics   42

Eighth Notes   20

1st & 2nd Endings   21

Forte (f)   42

Half Note   22

Half Rest   22

Half Step   32

Harmony   24

Hooked Bowing   41

Improvisation   47

Key Signature   15

Ledger Lines   10, 26

Measures   4

Measure Number   24

Moderato   20

Music Staff   4

Natural   32

Piano (p)   42

Pickup   30

Pizzicato (pizz.)   4

Quarter Note   4

Quarter Rest   4

Repeat Sign   5

Repeat Signs (enclosed)   22

Round   24

Scale   11

Shadow Bowing   13

Sharp   6

Slur   29

Solo   46

Staccato   40

Tempo Markings   20

Theme And Variations   35

Tie   29

Time Signature   5

Treble Clef   5 (violin)

Up Bow   13

Upbeat   30

Whole Note   37

Whole Rest   37

Whole Step   32

Composers

JOHANN SEBASTIAN BACH

• March in D   46

• Minuet No. 1   46

• Minuet No. 2   46

• Minuet in C   46

LUDWIG VAN BEETHOVEN

• Ode To Joy (from Sym. No. 9)   23

JOHANNES BRAHMS

• Academic Festival Overture Theme   39

FRANZ JOSEF HAYDN

• Surprise Symphony Theme   42

WOLFGANG AMADEUS MOZART

• A Mozart Melody   15

JACQUES OFFENBACH

• Can-Can From "Orpheus And The Underworld"   25

GIOACCHINO ROSSINI

• William Tell Overture   44

THOMAS TALLIS

• Tallis Canon   35

World Music

AFRICAN

• Tekele Lomeria   43

AMERICAN

• Arkansas Traveler   40

• Big Rock Candy Mountain   39

• Bile 'Em Cabbage Down   24

• Bluebird's Song   33

• Cripple Creek   43

• Grandparents Day   22

• Michael Row The Boat Ashore   22

• Old MacDonald Had A Farm   14

• Monday's Melody   37

• Pop Goes The Weasel   41

• Skip To My Lou   35

• Simple Gifts   45

• This Old Man   27

CARIBBEAN

• Banana Boat Song   30

ENGLISH

• Bingo   35

• English Round   25

• Sailor's Song   28

• Shepherd's Hey   39

FAR EASTERN

• Jingli Nona   31

FRENCH

• At Pierrot's Door   22

• Au Claire De La Lune   20

• French Folk Song   28

• Frére Jacques   24

MEXICAN

• Firoliralera   30

RUSSIAN

• Russian Folk Song   34

SLAVIC

• Morning Dance   8

WELSH

• Good King Wenceslas   9

TRADITIONAL HOLIDAY MUSIC

• Dreidel   13

• Jingle Bells   14

Teacher   The following may be photocopied and used as a student handout for instrument care.

TIPS FOR CARING FOR YOUR INSTRUMENT: WHAT TO DO AND WHAT NOT TO DO!

String instruments can last forever, but are easily damaged. To protect your instrument, be sure to follow these guidelines:

1. Never touch the bow hair, or the wooden part of the instrument with your hands.
2. Protect your instrument from extreme heat, cold, and quick temperature changes.
3. Wipe any rosin off your instrument with a soft cloth.
4. Place a cloth over your violin or viola before closing your case. Be sure to latch the case.
5. Loosen the bow hair after every use. Tighten it the same amount every time before playing.
6. Keep your instrument away from those who do not know how to properly care for it.
7. Do not attempt to repair your instrument. Tell your teacher or qualified music dealer if something needs to be fixed.

GUIDELINES FOR SELECTING THE CORRECT SIZED STRING INSTRUMENT FOR YOUR STUDENTS

Instrument	Size	Left Hand Span (Between pinky and index fingers)	Left Arm Length (From shoulder sleeve to end of middle finger)	Height
Violin	Full	5–6 inches	over 24 inches	
	3/4	4 1/2–5 inches	21–24 inches	
	1/2	4–4 1/2 inches	18–21 inches	
	1/4	3 1/2–4 inches	under 18 inches	
*Viola	16 inch	6 inches or more	28 inches or more	
	15 1/2 inch	6 inches	26–27 inches	
	15 inch	5–6 inches	25 inches	
	14 inch	5–6 inches	24 inches	
	13 1/4 inch	4 1/2–5 inches	21–24 inches	
Cello	Full	6 inches	24 inches	60 inches
	3/4	5 inches	22 inches	56 inches
	1/2	4 inches	20 inches	52 inches
	1/4	3 inches	18 inches	48 inches
Bass	3/4	6 1/2 inches	24 inches	over 60 inches
	1/2	5 3/4 inches	22 inches	56 inches
	1/4	5 inches	20 inches	52 inches

* A 3/4 violin and a junior viola are the same length. A full size violin is the same length as an intermediate viola.

Teacher   This keyboard diagram can be used as a visual aid to help you explain to your students half steps and whole steps. You may make photocopies of this keyboard for use by your students.

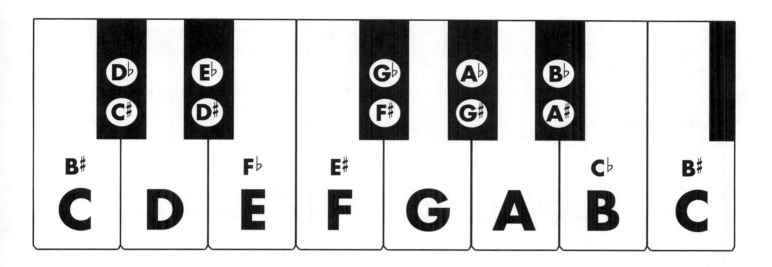

WORDS TO FAMILIAR MELODIES

The following are words to some of the familiar melodies that appear throughout this method. They are provided as a resource when teaching students to play the melodies on their string instruments.

Hot Cross Buns
Hot cross buns! Hot cross buns!
One, a pen-ny, Two, a pen-ny, Hot cross buns!

Michael Row the Boat Ashore
Mi-chael, row the boat a shore, Al-le-lu-ya
Mi-chael, row the boat a shore, Al-le-lu-ya.

Sis-ter, help to trim the sail, Al-le-lu-ya
Sis-ter, help to trim the sail, Al-le-lu-ya.

Mi-chael's boat is a gos-pel boat, Al-le-lu-ya
Mi-chael's boat is a gos-pel boat, Al-le-lu-ya.

Jor-dan's riv-er is chill-y and cold, Al-le-lu-ya
Jor-dan's riv-er is chill-y and cold, Al-le-lu-ya.

Jor-dan's riv-er is deep and wide, Al-le-lu-ya
Meet my moth-er on the oth-er side, Al-le-lu-ya.

Good King Wenceslas
Good King Wen-ces-las looked out,
On the feast of Ste-phen,
When the snow lay 'round a-bout,
deep and crisp and e-ven.

Old MacDonald
Old MacDonald had a farm, E-I-E-I-0
And on his farm he had a cow, E-I-E-I-0
With a moo-moo here, and a moo-moo there
Here a moo, there a moo
Everywhere a moo-moo
Old MacDonald had a farm, E-I-E-I-0.

Old MacDonald had a farm, E-I-E-I-0
And on his farm he had a pig, E-I-E-I-0
With a snort, snort here, and snort, snort there
Here a snort, there a snort
Everywhere a snort, snort
With a moo-moo here, and a moo-moo there
Here a moo, there a moo
Everywhere a moo-moo
Old MacDonald had a farm, E-I-E-I-0.

Pop Goes the Weasel
Round and round the cobbler's bench
The monkey chased the weasel,
The monkey thought 'twas all in fun
Pop! Goes the weasel.

Dreidel
I have a little dreidel
I made it out of clay
And when it's dry and ready
Then dreidel I shall play.

Chorus:
Dreidel, dreidel, dreidel
I made it out of clay
Dreidel, dreidel, dreidel
Then dreidel I shall play.

This Old Man
This old man, he played one
He played knick-knack on my thumb
Knick-knack paddywhack, give your dog a bone
This old man came rolling home.

This old man, he played two
He played knick-knack on my shoe
Knick-Knack paddywhack, give your dog a bone
This old man came rolling home.

Long, Long Ago
Tell me the tales
That to me were so dear,
Long, long ago,
Long, long ago:
Sing me the songs
I delighted to hear,
Long, long ago,
Long ago.

Jingle Bells
Jingle bells, jingle bells
Jingle all the way
Oh what fun it is to ride
In a one-horse open sleigh.
O Jingle bells, jingle bells
Jingle all the way
Oh what fun it is to ride
In a one-horse open sleigh.

Teacher   The following are standards established by the American String Teachers Association with the National School Orchestra Association for successful string/orchestra teaching in the schools. Use the standards as goals and guidelines in evaluating and developing your teaching skills.

AMERICAN STRING TEACHERS ASSOCIATION with NATIONAL SCHOOL ORCHESTRA ASSOCIATION

STANDARDS FOR SUCCESSFUL SCHOOL STRING/ORCHESTRA TEACHING

I. As a Musician

1. demonstrates a high level of musicianship in performance

2. performs at an intermediate to advanced level on at least one string instrument

3. demonstrates at least basic to intermediate performance concepts on one string instrument and understands advanced and artistic concepts on other string instruments

4. demonstrates ability to play by ear and improvise

5. demonstrates a basic knowledge of performing and teaching the woodwind, brass, and percussion instruments at least at a basic level, with an understanding of intermediate to advanced concepts

6. demonstrates orchestral conducting skills

7. demonstrates keyboard skills of at least a basic to intermediate level and accompanies melodies using at least I-IV-V chords

8. demonstrates aural discrimination skills

9. demonstrates the understanding of prevention of performance injuries

10. demonstrates the knowledge of a wide range of music repertoire for teaching diverse styles, genres, cultures and historical periods

II. As an Educator

1. understands and applies pedagogy for violin, viola, cello and bass

2. demonstrates effective rehearsal techniques for string and full orchestra

3. demonstrates the knowledge of a variety of string and orchestral instruction materials at all levels

4. demonstrates the knowledge of repertoire for student performance, including solo literature, orchestra music, and chamber music

5. demonstrates skill in arranging music for school orchestras

6. demonstrates strategies for integrating music with other disciplines

7. understands different student learning styles, levels of maturation, special needs, and adapts instruction accordingly

8. demonstrates knowledge of comprehensive, sequential K-12 music curricula, including string and orchestra, with appropriate goals and expectations for all levels of proficiencies

9. demonstrates understanding of the principles of a variety of homogeneous and heterogeneous pedagogical approaches for teaching string classes (Suzuki, Rolland, Bornoff, e.g.)

10. exhibits effective classroom management skills and strategies

11. demonstrates understanding of how to teach students of diverse ages, socio-economic, ethnic, and geographic backgrounds

12. demonstrates effective methods of assessing and evaluating student achievement

13. knows about instrument rental and purchasing

14. knows current technology for instruction, research, and musical applications

15. knows of current music and general education policies, including current scheduling practices for successful string and orchestra programs

16. demonstrates ability to gather pertinent orchestra program data

17. understands the importance of maintaining a balance between personal and career interests

18. demonstrates ability to develop budgets for equipment and supplies

19. demonstrates understanding of effective advocacy strategies for comprehensive music programs which include string/orchestra programs

20. demonstrates clear communication in written and oral form

21. demonstrates understanding of the K-12 National Music Education Standards and other state and local standards for music

III. As a Professional

A. Musician

1. continues to perform

2. demonstrates concepts and understandings necessary for student achievement of Grade 12 National Music Education Standards

3. exhibits effective, on-going professional self-assessment

4. continues to pursue opportunities for learning as a musician

B. Professional Affiliations and Related Activities

1. maintains active involvement in professional associations, such as MENC, ASTA/NSOA, SSA, CMA

2. continues to interact with other music educators, observes other programs

3. demonstrates professional ethics, appearance, behavior, and relationships within the profession, the school, and greater community

4. participates in ongoing professional development to improve teaching effectiveness

5. serves in leadership roles with state and local MEA's, ASTA/NSOA chapters

C. School and Community Relations

1. develops a healthy rapport with school administrators for nurturing a successful string and orchestra program

2. understands the value of positive interaction with other members of the music and arts community

3. establishes and maintains positive relations with school administrators, staff, and fellow teachers through communication and dialogue

4. articulates the positive aspects of the string/orchestra component of a school music program through writing and speaking

5. communicates effectively with parent support/booster groups, including clear and grammatically correct communication

6. advocates effectively for a strong school orchestra program

Teacher   The following bibliography lists the resources considered essential by the Professional String Teaching and Playing Association (ASTA with NSOA).

AMERICAN STRING TEACHERS ASSOCIATION with the NATIONAL SCHOOL ORCHESTRA ASSOCIATION

ESSENTIAL RESOURCE LIST FOR STRING TEACHERS

Stringed Instruments: Instruction and Study

The Complete String Guide: Standards, Programs, Purchase, and Maintenance. (1988). Reston, VA: Music Educators National Conference.

Dillon, J. & Kriechbaum, C. (1978). How to Design and Teach a Successful School String and Orchestra Program. San Diego, CA: Kjos West.

Dillon-Krass, J. & Straub, D. A. (Compilers). (1991). TIPS: Establishing a String and Orchestra Program. Reston, VA: Music Educators National Conference.

Green, E. A. (1966). Teaching Stringed Instruments in Classes. Englewood Cliff, NJ: Prentice-Hall, Inc. (available through ASTA).

Guidelines for Performances of School Music Groups: Expectations and Limitations. (1986) Reston, VA: Music Educators National Conference.

A Guide to Teaching Strings. Dubuque, IA: Wm. C. Brown and Co.

Mullins, S. (1998). Teaching Music: The Human Experience. Dallas, TX: Tarrant Dallas Printing.

Teaching String Instruments: A Course of Study. (1991). MENC Task Force on String Education. Reston, VA: Music Educators National Conference.

Highlights from the ASTA School Teacher's Forum. (1984-1994). Bloomington, IN: Tichenor Publishing.

String Syllabus. (revised 1997). ASTA. Bloomington, IN: Tichenor Publishing.

Straub, D. A., Bergonzi, L., & Witt, A. C. (Eds.). (1996). Strategies for Teaching Strings and Orchestra. Reston, VA: Music Educators National Conference.

Young, P. (1978). Playing the String Game - Strategies for Teaching Cello and Strings. Ann Arbor, MI: Shar Music.

Young, P. (1985). The String Play - The Drama of Playing and Teaching Strings. Austin, TX: University of Texas Press.

Strings, Winds, Brass, and Percussion
Managing the Instrumental Music Program

Colwell, R. J. and Goolsby, T. (1992). The Teaching of Instrumental Music. Englewood Cliffs, NJ: Prentice Hall.

Kohut, D. L. (1973). Instrumental Music Pedagogy: Teaching Techniques for School Band and Orchestra Directors. Englewood Cliffs, NJ: Prentice-Hall.

Strategies for Success in the Band and Orchestra. (1994). Reston, VA: Music Educators National Conference.

Walker, D. E. (1988). Teaching Music: Managing the Successful Music Program. New York, NY: Schirmer Books.

String Class Materials

Method Books

Allen, M., Gillespie, R., & Hayes, P.T. Essential Elements for Strings, (1995) Books I, II, and the Teacher Resource Kit, and Essential Techniques for Strings. Milwaukee, WI: Hal Leonard Corporation.

Anderson, G. & Frost, R. (1986). All for Strings. Kjos. Supplementary materials available.

Applebaum, S. Applebaum String Method. Books I, II, III. New York, NY: Belwin-Mills. Books I - III. Supplementary Applebaum materials include the following: Etudes for Technique and Musicianship, Chamber Music for Two String Instruments, Chamber Music for String Orchestra, and Solos with Piano Accompaniment.

Dabczynski, A., Meyer, R., & Philiips, B. (2002). String Explorer. Books I and II. Highland/Etling Pub. (a division of Alfred Music Publishing).

Dillon, J., Kjelland, J. & O'Reilly, J. Strictly Strings. Books I, II and III. Highland/Etling Pub. (a division of Alfred Music Publishing). Supplementary materials available.

Etling, F. String Method, Books I and II; Intermediate String Techniques; Solo Time for Strings, Books I, II, III, IV, and V; Workbook for Strings, Books I and II.

Froseth & Johnson (1981). Introducing the Strings, G.I.A. Publications.

Frost, R., & Fischbach, G. (2002). Artistry in Strings. Books I and II. San Diego, CA: Neil A. Kjos Music Company.

Gazda, D. & Stoutamire, A. (1997). Spotlight on Strings. San Diego, CA: Neil A. Kjos Music Company.

Isaac, M. (1962) String Class Method. Chicago, IL: M. M. Cole. Books I and II.

Matesky, R. & Womack, A. (1971). Learn to Play a Stringed Instrument. New York, NY: Alfred Music Co. Books I, II, and III.

Matesky, R. Learn to Play in the Orchestra. (1971). New York, NY: Alfred Music Co. Volumes I and II

Muller, F. & Rusch, H. Muller-Rusch String Method. (1961). Books I - V plus supplementary materials: ensembles, solos, etc. San Diego, CA: Neil A. Kjos Music Co.

Music Lists for Orchestra/String Orchestra

Non-Graded:

Farrish, M. K. (1965). String Music in Print. New York, NY: R. R. Bowker.

Farrish, M. K. (1968). Supplement to String Music in Print. New York, NY: R. R. Bowker.

Farrish, M. K. (1979). Orchestral Music in Print: Educational Section. Philadelphia, PA: Musicdata.

Littrell, D. & Racin, L. (2001) Teaching Music Through Performance in Orchestra. Chicago, IL: GIA Publications, Inc.

Graded Lists:

Matesky, R. & Smith, J. (1979). ASTA - NSOA Compendium of Orchestra & String Orchestra Literature: 1959-1977. Reston, VA: American String Teachers Association.

Mayer, F. R. (Ed.). (1993). The String Orchestra Super List. Reston, VA: Music Educators National Conference.

National School Orchestra Association - Sure-Fire Materials for the First-Year Orchestra Director.

NOTE: *Many state organizations have graded music lists available.*

National Standards for Arts Education

Allen, M. L. (1995). "The national standards for arts education: Implications for school string programs." American String Teacher, 45 (2), 30.

Bergonzi, L. (1996). "School teachers: The national standards in music: Access to string study for all children." American String Teacher, 46 (2), 69.

Dabczynski, A. H. (1995). "National standards for arts education: A golden opportunity for string teachers." American String Teacher, 45 (1), 73.

Daugherty, E. (1995). "Editorial: Implementing national standards in music: Context challenges and opportunities." The Quarterly of the Center for Research in Music Education, 6 (2), 3.

Kjelland, J. (1995). "String teacher preparation and the national music standards." American String Teacher, 45 (4), 34.

Mark, M. L. (1995). "Music education and the national standards: A historical review." The Quarterly of the Center for Research in Music Education, 6 (2), 34.

National Standards for Arts Education: What Every Young American Should Know and Be Able to Do in the Arts. Reston, VA: Music Educators National Conference.

Opportunity-to-Learn Standards for Music Instruction: Grades Pre K-12. (1994) Reston, VA: Music Educators National Conference.

Performance Standards for Music: Strategies and Benchmarks for Assessing Progress Toward the National Standards, Grades Pre K-12. (1996) Reston, VA: Music Educators National Conference.

The School Music Program: A New Vision. (1994). Reston, VA: Music Educators National Conference.

Shuler, S. C. (1995). "The impact of national standards on the preparation, in-service professional development, and assessment of music teachers." Arts Education Policy Review, 96 (3), 2.

Straub, D. A. (1995). "The national standards for art education: context and issues." American String Teacher, 45 (3), 24. Straub, D. A., Bergonzi, L., & Witt, A. C. (Eds.) (1996) Strategies for Teaching Strings and Orchestra. Reston, VA: Music Educators National Conference.

Advocacy

Action Kit for Music Education. (1991). Reston, VA: Music Educators National Conference. (brochures, books, videos)

Does Your School District Have an Orchestra Program? (1993). Reston, VA: Music Educators National Conference. (brochure)

Day, S. H. (1996). "Teaching orchestra on a year-round schedule." Teaching Music, 4, 33-35.

Kendall, S. (1997). "Securing our string programs." American String Teacher, 47 (2), 47.

Tellejohn, P. (1989). "Ensure your string program's success." American String Teacher, 76 (2), 30-32.

Scheduling Time for Music. (1995). Reston, VA: Music Educators National Conference.

Pedagogical Videos

From University of Wisconsin, Division of University Outreach, Department of Continuing Education.

Rabin, M. , et al. (1986). Rabin on Strings.

Rabin, M. & Smith, P. (1984). Guide to Orchestral Bowings Through Music Styles.

Paul Rolland

Rolland, P. Basic Principles of Violin Playing. (MENC Publication, 1959: ASTA, 1983).

Rolland, P. and Mutschler, M. (1974). The Teaching of Action in String Playing: Developmental and Remedial Techniques. Urbana, IL: Illinois String Research Associates.

Film

University of Illinois Film Series on Teaching of Action in String Playing. Urbana, IL: Illinois String Research Associates. Fourteen 16mm color films or videotapes; artists, teachers, and students demonstrate principles of Teaching of Action in String Playing.

String Repair

Bearden, L. & Bearden, D. (1972). Emergency String Repair Manual, 2nd Edition. AL: The University of Alabama Press.

Weisshaar, O. H. (1966). Preventative Maintenance of Stringed Instruments. Rockville Center, MD: Belwin, Inc.

Zurfluh, J. D. (Ed.). (1978). String Instrument Repair and Maintenance Manual. American String Teachers Association.

Bowing

Green, E. A. (1957). Orchestra Bowings and Routines - 2nd edition. (18th Printing). Reston, VA: American String Teachers Association.

Berman, J., Jackson and Sarah K. ASTA Dictionary of Bowing/Pizzicato Terms and Techniques (4th Edition). 1998. Bloomington, IN: Tichenor Publishing.

Video-Tape

Rabin, M. & Smith, P. (1991). Guide to Orchestral Bowings through Music Styles. Madison, WI: University of Wisconsin-Extension.

Pedagogical Concerns

From *American String Teacher*

Allen, M. L. (1994). "Introducing and integrating basic skills in the beginning string class." American String Teacher, 44 (3), 69-72.

Fischbach, G. "Getting from here to there with a smile: A sequential outline of the skills of shifting for business and pleasure." American String Teacher.
Three part article:
    I. Basic Principles, Summer 1980, 30 (3), 11-12.
    II. Sequential Course of Study. Autumn, 1980, 30 (4), 28-30.
    III. Shifting for Pleasure, Winter 1981, 31(1), 12-13.

Gillespie, R. (1997). "String teacher training: Using history to guide the future." American String Teacher, 47 (1), 62-66.

Moskovitz, M. D. (1997). "Making the connection: Shifting through hand positions." American String Teacher, 47 (3), 55-58.

From *The Instrumentalist*

Burgess, N. (1977). "Fiddling for technical development." The Instrumentalist. 32 (5), 81-83.

Gillespie, R. (1989). "Teaching spiccato to string classes: Effective strategies for teaching your group the spiccato bounce." The Instrumentalist, 44 (4), 52, 56, 59-60.

Gillespie, R. (1992). "Building a Bass Section." The Instrumentalist, 47 (5), 66-69.

Grieve, T. (1989). "Fresh approaches to scale practice." The Instrumentalist, 43 (7), 44-46.

Rejto, G. (1978). "Strings: Producing a beautiful string tone." The Instrumentalist, 33 (2), 76.

Journals

American String Teacher
American String Teachers Association (ASTA)
with the National School Orchestra Association (NSOA)
4153 Chain Bridge Road
Fairfax, VA 22030

The Instrumentalist
200 Northfield Road
Northfield, IL 60093

Music Educators Journal
Music Educators National Conference
1806 Robert Fulton Drive
Reston, VA 22091-4348

Teaching Music
Music Educators National Conference
1806 Robert Fulton Drive
Reston, VA 22091-4348

Professional Organizations

American String Teachers Association (ASTA) with the National School Orchestra
Association (NSOA)
4153 Chain Bridge Road
Fairfax, VA 22030
www.astaweb.com

Music Educators National Conference
1806 Robert Fulton Drive
Reston, VA 22091-4348
www.menc.org

Suzuki Association of the Americas
P.O. Box 17310
Boulder, CO 80308

Teacher   The following are video training programs for developing skills to diagnose and solve string students playing skills.

Video String Teacher Teaching Programs

Contact Robert Gillespie for these materials:
Ohio State University School of Music
110 Weigel Hall
1866 College Road
Columbus, OH 43210-1170
gillespie.5@osu.edu

Gillespie, Robert. The Violin Bowing Diagnostic Skills Program. Two videotapes and manual designed to train and evaluate teachers' abilities to recognize and solve common bowing problems of beginning violin students. Available for rent or purchase through the ASTA Media Resource Center.

Gillespie, Robert. The Violin Instrument Position and Left Hand Skills Training Program. A videotape and manual designed to train teachers to recognize common instrument position and left hand skills problems of beginning and intermediate violin students. Available for rent or purchase through the ASTA Media Resource Center.

Gillespie, Robert, William Conable, and Brent Wilson. The Cello Diagnostic Skills Training Program. A videotape and manual designed to train teachers to recognize common instrument position and left hand fingering problems of beginning and intermediate cello students. Available for rent or purchase through the ASTA Media Resource Center.

272

Authors

Professor of Music Education, Florida State University, Tallahassee, FL

ROBERT GILLESPIE
Professor of Music, The Ohio State University, Columbus, OH

PAMELA TELLEJOHN HAYES
Orchestra Coordinator (retired), Richland School District Two, Columbia, SC

JOHN HIGGINS
Managing Producer and Editor, Composer and Arranger, Hal Leonard Corp., Milwaukee, WI

Credits

Managing Editor and Producer	Paul Lavender
Production Editor	Stuart Malavsky
Orchestra Arrangements	John Higgins
Design and Art Direction	Richard Slater Tim Begonia
Music Engraving and Typesetting	Thomas Schaller
Play Along Trax Arrangements and Production	Paul Lavender John Higgins
Additional Arrangements	John Moss
Essential Elements Rhythm Section	Steve Millikan - Keyboards Steve Potts - Keyboards Steve Dokken - Bass Sandy Williams - Guitars Steve Hanna - Percussion Larry Sauer - Drums
Recording and Mixing Engineers Aire Born Studios, Indianapolis, IN	Mark Aspinall John Bolt David Price Ben Vawter Mike Wilson
Additional Recording Production	Jared Rodin Mark Aspinall
Project Supervision Aire Born Studios, Indianapolis, IN	Nanci Milam Mike Wilson Nina Hunt
Announcer	Scott Hoke

The authors wish to give special thanks to Herman Knoll Senior, Vice President of Hal Leonard,
for his dedication, leadership, and expertise in the creation of the Essential Elements educational program.